SUSHI SLIM

PHOTOGRAPHY
BY
LISA LINDER

BY
MAKIKO
SANO

THE COUNTRYMAN PRESS · WOODSTOCK · V.T.

Contents

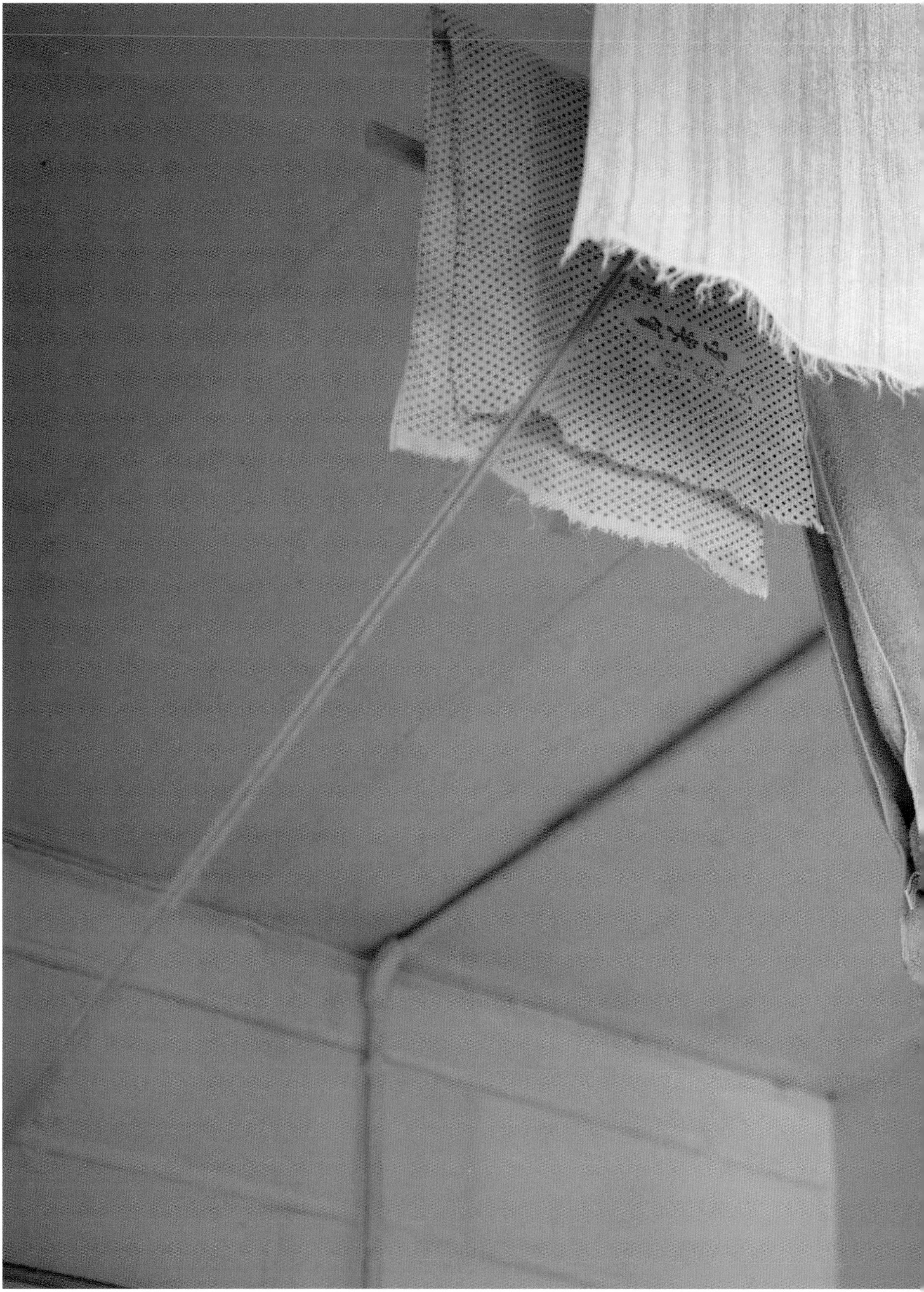

寿司スリム法

How to Sushi Slim

Virtuous indulgence

Indulge and slim

Japanese food is healthy, delicious, good for you, and helps you lose weight. For women in Japan, how, what, and when they eat is seated in tradition, in the treasured ingredients of rice, miso, wasabi, fish, tea, and seaweed that are the traditional harvests of our island nation. All of these have incredible slimming and beauty-boosting benefits.

The sushi, soup, salad, and bento box recipes in this book are not only the height of food fashion, but also the perfect fast food for busy people on the run ... and you will learn how simple they are to make.

And although people in the West might view the phrase "healthy diet" with trepidation, bringing as it does connotations of abstinence and avoidance, our style of healthy eating is all about what I call Virtuous Indulgence. Japanese food is full of all the sensuous experiences you would normally feel deprived of on a western "diet." We eat first with our eyes: the food looks beautiful. Next up come touch, feel, and texture, and finally the exquisite taste.

The Japanese culture of slimness

In Japan, we are taught from a really young age what is good for our bodies. It's part of our culture to eat healthy foods which help maintain a trim figure and improve our looks.

Unlike the Western sweep-it-under-the-carpet approach to weight gain, Japanese women openly scrutinize each other's figures and won't hesitate to mention if someone has added a few pounds. In fact it has even been legislated for, with the maximum waist size for a woman over 40 years old set at 35 inches. Some of Tokyo's restaurants have scales at each table; others serve 500-calorie lunches.

We may not have calorie-counting restaurants in the West (yet!), but this book will do the work for you. Each of the delicious dishes has been calorie counted, and our dietitian-devised diet plan will show how, by introducing just one Japanese meal a day into your diet, you can lose a healthy amount of weight each week, or just maintain your ideal weight. So, if you want to indulge your way to a healthier, trimmer, more glowing you, try Sushi Slim.

Japanese food:
The facts and your figure

Many Japanese people are taught to eat until they are 80 percent full, and this might be one reason for their trim figures. In the latest world obesity rankings, Japan scored the second lowest percentage, with a mere 3.9 percent, compared to America's troubling 33.8 percent.

The average daily calorie intake in Japan is 2,754 kcal, compared to the USA's 3,825 kcal.

The Omega-3 content of the high prevalence of fish in the diet, along with a relatively small amount of meat eaten in Japan, is thought responsible for low levels of cardiovascular problems in the country.

They say variety is the spice of life. The typical Japanese person will have about 100 varieties of food per week, compared with just 30 in the average British diet, or 45 in the Mediterranean diet.

Results from a study at the end of 2011 suggested that a traditional Japanese diet may help to manage Type 2 diabetes mellitus.

For many years researchers have been aware of the extreme health and longevity benefits of a Japanese diet, especially the now legendary Okinawa way of eating, where inhabitants of the Japanese island regularly live to 100 (and an Okinawan was found to be 6.5 times less likely to die from breast cancer).

When you understand all that this cuisine offers, the only question about embracing a whole new style of eating is: why didn't I do it before?

Seven reasons why the Japanese diet will help you lose weight

1

Portion control

Because of the way in which it is presented, with three or four dishes, Japanese meals give the impression of being bigger than they are. At least one of the dishes will be a low-calorie, filling soup. In Western cuisine, the style is to use one big dinner plate groaning with quite a mountain of food. A typical set of sushi contains about 300 calories. An average Western plate of food can be 500 calories *more* than this.

2

Chopsticks

Slowing the rate at which you eat allows your brain to notice when you feel full. The Western eat-on-the-run way of dining means we have often overeaten before we even know it. Japanese people find it easier to notice when we are full because we use chopsticks, which are a more time-consuming way to eat. Set aside at least 20 minutes to eat each meal, as it takes your stomach about that time to register fullness.

3

Swerve dairy and meat

Japanese people do eat some meat, but not much of it compared to the Western diet. Also, dairy wasn't eaten in a traditional Japanese diet, and still isn't a big part of it. These two food stuffs are high in fat and responsible for much of the Western daily calorie intake.

4 四 Big breakfasts and early, light suppers

We often eat a selection of dishes in the morning: miso soup; rice; omelet; and broiled salmon (see page 76 if you'd like to try a Japanese breakfast). Japanese people also tend not to snack after 4pm, and eat an early supper that focuses on fish and vegetables. We also don't tend to eat desserts at home.

5 五 Green tea

Japanese people drink green tea throughout the day and it's readily available from street vending machines, which preheat it in cans. It contains virtually no calories. In contrast, the western equivalent—the ubiquitous coffee shop—is a diet baddie. Even if you order a skinny latte, you will take in around 100 calories, and that can increase to a staggering 500 calories for a mocha with cream.

6 六 Good things in small packages

Instead of tearing open a long roll of cookies and ploughing through them, Japanese people tend to pick up snack-sized dainties. Small packaging minimizes the temptation to overdo it. So, if you're wavering and feeling like you might blow your diet, pick up a mini pack of sesame snaps, or satisfyingly salty rice crackers. It's a simple idea, but a great damage limitation exercise.

7 七 Acid test

Sushi translates as "vinegared rice." Vinegar and other acetic acid-based pickles, ubiquitous in Japanese food, have a distinct effect on how we digest fat when eaten as part of a meal. Japanese researchers recently found that acetic acid may aid in fat burning. Another study found that vinegar taken after a high-GI food, such as white bread, not only reduced peaks in blood glucose, but also increased the feeling of fullness. When vinegar was introduced into a test diet, 10 percent less body fat was produced.

Diamond ingredients

"Our foods are full of goodies. We say eating them makes us sparkle like diamonds ... forever."

The Japanese diet not only helps you to lose pounds and maintain a healthy weight, it's anti-aging, bursting with complexion-boosting goodies, and adds gloss and condition to your hair and nails.

Part of what makes Japanese food so different is the myriad of "diamond" foods we use, that do so much more than taste great.

GINGER FOR ALL-ROUND HEALTH
This rhizome contains silicone to promote smooth and even skin tone, glossy hair, and healthy teeth and nails. It is also considered to act as a mild aphrodisiac.

NORI FOR MERMAID LOCKS
This is the seaweed used to make sushi. It is believed to stimulate hair growth as it contains naturally high quantities of biotin, a compound often sold as a supplement in health food stores to strengthen hair.

SESAME SEEDS FOR A YOUTHFUL BODY
These are small but nutritionally mighty. They have a cholesterol-lowering effect. Sesamin, a compound found in the seeds, has also been found to protect the liver from oxidative damage. The seeds are high in copper, which strengthens blood vessels to promote healthy skin and hair. Crush them in a mortar and pestle to release the maximum health-giving qualities.

VINEGAR
Japanese rice vinegar is used to flavor sushi rice. Several studies have found it can suppress body fat accumulation (see point 7, left).

YUZU FOR YOUNGER SKIN
This fragrant citrus contains antioxidants, bioflavanoids, and a high level of vitamin C (three times that of lemon). It's worth seeking out from Japanese stores, and use it in any of the recipes in the book that call for lemon or lime. Yuzu zest also contains nomilin, a compound which has relaxing properties. Japanese women rely on it to rejuvenate maturing skin. I love to use the juice in salad dressings, or the zest shaved into a dipping sauce, or into the bath!

Diet-boosting drinks

As crucial as the food to the Japanese diet are the drinks. From skin-revitalizing soups to low-calorie tipples, what's in your glass or teacup could have more impact on your Sushi Slim plan than you think.

Green tea

Green tea is laden with antioxidants that help lower cholesterol

Green tea has antibacterial properties which sweeten the breath

Green tea—the most popular tea in my restaurant—wins hands down in the calorie stakes against the Western fascination with dairy-laden hot drinks. It is virtually calorie-free. In fact, you could actually burn about 80 calories for every five cups of green tea you drink, due to the "thermic effect" on the body of processing the drink.

We drink hot green tea with every meal, and even buy it ready-made in bottles. It also makes a refreshing drink served cold, over ice, in the warmer months.

Oolong tea

Japanese oolong tea is almost like our cup of coffee. More intensely flavored than green tea, I tend to have one very strong cup in the morning to provide that same boost that a shot of coffee would.

Barley tea

Strict dieters such as my sister would choose Japanese barley tea for its reputed detox properties, drinking it as we would drink water in the west.

Shochu and sake

Women in Japan opt for these over a cold beer, as they don't have any wheat content. The drinks have reputations for minimizing hangovers, and shochu has a mere 35 calories per 2-ounce shot. Sake, also low in calories, contains more than 20 kinds of amino acids. Among their benefits is slow aging of the skin.

Japanese wonder soups

FROM TOP: Chicken Collagen Soup in cube form; Hearty Root Vegetable miso soup

Collagen soup

You may have noticed little sachets of liquid collagen being sold at beauty counters. But this is old news in Japan. A girlfriend of mine first made me Collagen Soup in my teens and I've been hooked ever since. Even the morning after drinking it, my skin looks firmer and plumper. And it's not my imagination: The Japanese Journal of Complementary and Alternative Medicine found that drinks containing 10g of collagen produced a 50 percent observable effectiveness against wrinkles and skin dryness within one week. The soup I prefer is made with fish, either salmon or grouper, and it isn't something you will find at Japanese restaurants in the West. You can find recipes on pages 78–81. I eat it twice a week. I often make a large batch and freeze it in cubes to use later.

Miso soup

In Japan we would quite happily have miso at every meal. I carry sachets of it in my handbag to have at my desk. There are many different ways to make the soup, so it never gets boring (see pages 72–75). Miso has high levels of umami—the savory taste—and so is hugely appealing and very satisfying.

Miso contains only 30 calories per 1-cup serving

The amino acids in miso help rid the body of harmful toxins

Miso has high levels of antioxidants, the goodies that clean up the "free radical" cells responsible for aging

Miso is rich in zinc and manganese, which help give glossy hair and healthy nails

Sushi Slim meal plan

Miki Symons MSc, Japanese-trained dietitian

I have devised three diet plans. Each replaces just one meal a day in a normal Western diet with a delicious Japanese meal from Sushi Slim (though you can swap in two meals a day if you want ... and it's easy to get hooked!).

On the Sushi Slim plan, you should aim to lose no more than two pounds each week. A slow, steady weight loss, along with taking regular exercise, is the best way to long-term success. Crash diets never work. It is also important to eat a morning and an afternoon snack, to keep you feeling full and avoiding temptation.

I advise that everyone considering a weight-loss diet should check with their physician first, just to rule out any problems. And always remember to drink lots of water throughout the day.

How many calories you should eat each day depends on your current weight, height and whether you are aiming to lose weight, or simply maintain your figure. According to the U.S. Department of Health and Human Services:

In general, eating plans containing 1,000 to 1,200 calories will help most women to lose weight safely.

Eating plans between 1,200 calories and 1,600 calories each day are suitable for men and may also be appropriate for women who weigh 165 pounds or more, or who exercise regularly.

For more details, or to calculate your recommended calorie intake, go to http://www.nhlbi.nih.gov/health/public/heart/obesity/aim_hwt.pdf.

You should remember that, as you slim, and move to maintaining weight, you can increase your calorie intake.

I have given plans for 1,300 calories, 1,500 calories, and 1,700 calories. I have also given calorie counts for every meal, in case you need to fine-tune your daily calorie target. I have rounded off all calorie counts to the nearest five calories, for ease.

CHOOSE FROM:

1,300 kcal/day

300 kcal breakfast

CEREAL AND TOAST
Cup of coffee or tea with lowfat milk **+15kcal**
1¼-ounce bowl of cereal or oatmeal with lowfat milk **+150kcal**
Thin slice of whole wheat toast **+60kcal**
½ tablespoon jam **+25 kcal**
1 teaspoon butter **+35 kcal**

FRUIT AND YOGURT
Cup of coffee or tea with lowfat milk **+15kcal**
3½-ounce pot fat-free yogurt **+70kcal**
3½ ounces mango **+65 kcal**
3½ ounces pineapple **+55 kcal**
1 cup raspberries **+40 kcal**
5 ounces melon **+50 kcal**

EGG AND BACON
Cup of coffee or tea with lowfat milk **+15kcal**
Thin slice of whole wheat toast **+60 kcal**
1 teaspoon butter **+35 kcal**
2 small poached eggs **+120 kcal**
2 slices of broiled Canadian bacon **+70 kcal**

100 kcal snack

Green tea **+0 kcal**
Small banana **+75kcal**
Handful of strawberries, about 5 **+25kcal**
OR
Green tea **+0 kcal**
Medium handful of almonds, about 10 **+70kcal**
1 medium satsuma **+30kcal**

500 kcal lunch

Sushi Slim options

BENTO BOX LUNCHES
Unlimited green tea **+0 kcal**
Bento Box (choose from 10 different boxes) **all +460–510 kcal**

SUSHI LUNCH —*2 choices*
Unlimited green tea **+0 kcal**
Monk Rolls, 4 pieces **+510 kcal**

Unlimited green tea **+0 kcal**
Basic Miso Soup **+30 kcal**
Tempura King Shrimp and Avocado inside-out rolls, 6 pieces **+460 kcal**

COLLAGEN SOUP LUNCH
Unlimited green tea **+0 kcal**
1 bowl Chicken Collagen Soup, with shredded chicken **+300 kcal**
1 portion Lightly Grilled Tuna with Arugula **+165kcal**
handful of strawberries (about 10) **+50 kcal**

Western options

SANDWICH AND SOUP
Small cheese salad sandwich **+300 kcal**
Vegetable and bean soup **+190 kcal**

RAMEN NOODLES
Broiled salmon ramen soup noodles **+465 kcal**

TOASTIE, SALAD, AND FRUIT
1 slice cheese on toast with 1½ ounces cheddar, plus large mixed salad with 2 teaspoons dressing **+300 kcal**
large apple **+100 kcal**
medium banana **+100 kcal**

SALAD AND YOGURT POT
Tuna Niçoise salad with dressing **+300 kcal**
4-ounce yogurt and granola pot **+185 kcal**

300 kcal dinner

Sushi Slim options

SUSHI —*6 choices*
Tuna and Cucumber inside-out rolls, 6 pieces **+335 kcal**
Red and Yellow Pepper, Onion, and Mushroom gunkan, 6 pieces **+290 kcal**
Avocado and Chili hosomaki rolls, 6 pieces **+300 kcal**
Crab Stick and Lettuce hosomaki rolls, 6 pieces **+255 kcal**
Salmon nigiri, 6 pieces **+ 330 kcal**
Avocado nigiri, 6 pieces **+320 kcal**

SOUP AND SALAD —*2 choices*
Tofu and Seaweed Miso Soup **+45 kcal**
1 portion Tuna and Avocado Tartare **+230 kcal**
Eggplant miso soup **+35 kcal**
2 portions of Steamed Vegetables with Creamy Tofu Dressing **+220 kcal**

Western options

OMELET AND SALAD
Omelet made with 2 eggs, 1 teaspoon oil, and 1 tablespoon chopped ham **+225 kcal**
Mixed salad (unlimited amount) with 2 teaspoons dressing **+75 kcal**

PASTA AND SAUCE
2 ounces (raw weight) pasta **+175 kcal**
3½ ounces Bolognese sauce (made with lean ground meat) **+140 kcal**
OR
3 ounces (raw weight) pasta **+260 kcal**
4 ounces tomato sauce **+50 kcal**
Plus unlimited steamed vegetables **+negligible kcal**

BROILED CHICKEN AND VEG
1 large chicken breast **+130 kcal**
1 small eggplant **+20 kcal** plus 1 red bell pepper **+50 kcal** roasted with 1 tablespoon olive oil **+120 kcal**

CURRY AND RICE
1 cup cooked brown rice **+200 kcal**
3½ ounces vegetable curry **+100 kcal**
Plus unlimited steamed vegetables **+negligible kcal**

CHOOSE FROM:

1,500 kcal/day

400 kcal breakfast

EGGS
Cup of coffee or tea with lowfat milk
+15kcal
Scrambled eggs made with 3 large
eggs **+225 kcal** and 1 teaspoon butter
+35 kcal
1 medium slice whole wheat toast
+85 kcal
with 1 teaspoon butter **+35 kcal**

**FRUIT, NUTS, SEEDS, AND
YOGURT**
Cup of coffee or tea with lowfat milk
+15kcal
¾ cup 2% Greek yogurt **+150kcal**
7 ounces fresh fruit salad **+115kcal**
1 ounce nuts and seed mix **+150kcal**

TOAST AND APPLE
Cup of coffee or tea with lowfat milk
+15kcal
2 medium slices whole wheat toast
+170kcal
2 teaspoons butter **+70kcal**
1 tablespoon jam **+50kcal**
1 small apple **+90kcal**

100 kcal snack

Unlimited green tea **+0 kcal**
Small banana **+75kcal**
Medium satsuma **+30kcal**
OR
Unlimited green tea **+0 kcal**
Tofu and Seaweed miso soup **+45kcal**
Large handful of strawberries, about 10
+50kcal

500 kcal lunch

Sushi Slim options

BENTO BOX LUNCHES
Unlimited green tea **+0 kcal**
Bento Box (choose from 10 different
boxes) all **+460 –510 kcal**

SUSHI LUNCH —*2 choices*
Unlimited green tea **+0 kcal**
Avocado and Chili hosomaki rolls,
6 pieces **+300 kcal**
Oil-Free Edamame, about 30 pods
+50 kcal
7 ounces tropical fruit salad **+145 kcal**
Unlimited green tea **+0 kcal**
Tempura King Shrimp and Avocado
inside-out roll, 6 pieces **+460 kcal**
Basic Miso Soup **+30 kcal**

COLLAGEN SOUP LUNCH
Unlimited green tea **+0 kcal**
Chicken Collagen Soup, with
shredded chicken **+300 kcal**
1 portion Eggplant and Shallot Salad
+156 kcal
1 cup raspberries **+60 kcal**

Western options

SANDWICH AND SOUP
Hummus and vegetable sandwich
+400 kcal
Tomato and vegetable soup, without
dairy **+100 kcal**

PIZZA AND SALAD
½ medium (8-inch) margherita pizza
+410 kcal
Salad with 2 teaspoons dressing
+75 kcal

WRAP AND FRUIT
Chargrilled chicken wrap **+410 kcal**
1 small apple **+90 kcal**

SALAD AND MUFFIN
Tuna salad with reduced-calorie
dressing **+200 kcal**
Low-fat blueberry muffin **+300 kcal**

400 kcal dinner

Sushi Slim options

SUSHI—*3 choices*
3 Hint of Lime hand rolls **+410 kcal**
2 Suzu Yellowtail hand rolls **+405 kcal**
8 pieces mixed fish nigiri
about +400 kcal

SOUP AND SALAD—*2 choices*
1 portion Lightly Grilled Tuna with
Arugula **+165kcal**
1 portion Facelift-in-a-Bowl
+210kcal

Spicy Pork miso soup **+100kcal**
1 portion Steamed Sesame Chicken
Salad **+245kcal**

Western options

**BROILED FISH AND ROASTED
VEGETABLES**
4-ounce salmon fillet, broiled
+250kcal
7 ounces mixed roast vegetables
+130kcal

**GNOCCHI WITH TOMATO
AND OLIVE SAUCE**
5 ounces plain gnocchi **+230kcal**
3½ ounces tomato and olive pasta
sauce **+150kcal**

**COUSCOUS AND VEGETABLE
TAGINE**
¾ cup cooked couscous **+175kcal**
14 ounces vegetable tagine **+220kcal**

BAKED POTATO AND CHEESE
1 medium baked potato **+160kcal**
½ cup grated cheddar cheese
+250kcal

CHOOSE FROM:

1,700 kcal/day

500 kcal breakfast

LATTE AND BACON ROLL
Large whole milk latte (no syrup, no cream) **+135kcal**
Brown bread roll **+145kcal**
3 slices of broiled Canadian bacon **+105kcal**
2 teaspoons butter **+70kcal**

CEREAL AND TOAST
Cup of coffee or tea with lowfat milk **+15kcal**
1-ounce bowl of cereal or oatmeal with lowfat milk **+150kcal**
2 medium slices whole wheat toast **+170kcal**
2 teaspoons butter **+70kcal**
1 tablespoon jam **+50kcal**

HAM, CHEESE, AND RYE BREAD
Cup of coffee or tea with lowfat milk **+15kcal**
3 slices rye bread **+165kcal**
2 slices emmental cheese **+240kcal**
3 ounces smoked or unsmoked ham **+80kcal**

100 kcal snack

Unlimited green tea **+0 kcal**
Large handful of almonds, about 15 **+100kcal**
OR
Unlimited green tea **+0 kcal**
Basic Miso Soup **+30 kcal**
Large handful of cherries, about 10 **+70kcal**

500 kcal lunch

Sushi Slim options

BENTO BOX LUNCHES
Unlimited green tea **+0 kcal**
Bento Box (choose from 10 different boxes) **all +460–510 kcal**

HOSOMAKI FEAST
Crab Stick and Lettuce, 6 pieces **+255 kcal**
Canned Tuna and Scallion, 6 pieces **+245 kcal**

CHILI HEAD
Spicy Salmon inside-out rolls, 6 pieces **+450 kcal**
Basic Miso Soup **+30 kcal**

OMEGA-3 HIT
2 x Omega-3 Hit hand rolls **+445 kcal**
Basic Miso Soup **+30 kcal**

Western options

BIG TOASTIE
Sandwich chain large cheese and onion toastie **+500 kcal**

CHEESE SALAD PACK
Feta, lentil, and rice salad **+520 kcal**

RAMEN NOODLES
Large bowl chicken ramen **+520 kcal**

LETTUCE WRAP "BURGER"
Beef burger wrapped in lettuce, without bread **+475 kcal**

500 kcal dinner

Sushi Slim options

FACELIFT SOUP AND SUSHI
1 bowl Facelift-in-a-Bowl **+210 kcal**
Okra pods and Sesame inside-out rolls, 6 pieces **295 kcal**

SALAD
Fill-You-Up Soba Noodle Salad **+500 kcal**

JAPANESE BREAKFAST-FOR-DINNER
Fish, rice, omelet, miso soup, pickles **+560 kcal**

TERIYAKI AND RICE
1 portion Chicken Teriyaki **+195 kcal**
1 cup cooked brown rice **+220 kcal**
Plus unlimited steamed vegetables **+negligible kcal** with 2 teaspoons butter **+70kcal**

Western options

ROAST VEGETABLES WITH RICE AND FRUIT SALAD
12 ounces roast vegetable salad **+220 kcal**
1 cup cooked brown rice **+200 kcal**
7 ounces fresh fruit salad **+85 kcal**

CHICKEN CURRY
4 ounces dry tandoori chicken **+240 kcal**
1 cup cooked brown rice **+200 kcal**
1 tablespoon mango chutney **+60 kcal**

STIR-FRIED SHRIMP AND VEGETABLES
1 portion, made with splash of oil **+300 kcal**
6 ounces cooked rice noodles **+190 kcal**

STEAK AND SALAD
6-ounce sirloin steak **+240 kcal**
baked sweet potato **+175 kcal**
2 teaspoons French dressing **+75kcal**
Unlimited green salad **+negligible kcal**

FOOLPROOF SUSHI

きほん

How to make perfect sushi rice
How to cut vegetables
How to choose and cut fish
Secrets of a Japanese pantry

HOW TO MAKE PERFECT SUSHI RICE

2¾ cups short-grain sushi rice
½ cup seasoned rice vinegar

You will need a large, shallow bowl, or an oven tray or large serving plate.

HOW TO COOK RICE

Find a large pan with a tight-fitting lid. Wash the rice thoroughly, then let dry in a strainer for at least 30 minutes.

Measure 3 cups of water and pour it into your pan. Add the rice. Place over medium heat, cover, and leave it for 10 to 13 minutes, until it comes to a boil (listen for the bubbles; do not remove the lid).

When the water has come to a boil, reduce the heat to its lowest for 30 seconds, then turn the heat off. Leave it for 15 minutes with the lid on.

Now it's ready.

HOW TO SEASON SUSHI RICE

Put the hot rice in your bowl, tray, or other container, sprinkle on the rice seasoning vinegar fairly evenly and mix it in gently but really well with a broad wooden or plastic spoon or spatula.

Cool it down with a fan, turning the rice carefully, to let every grain of rice soak up all the vinegar.

Leave it for 10 to 15 minutes until the rice is cool to the touch, but not too cold.

You are now ready to make sushi, or to freeze the rice in handy portion sizes.

MAKING BROWN SUSHI RICE

You can make brown sushi rice with exactly the same quantities and method. The only difference is that brown sushi rice needs to be soaked.

Soak it in the measured amount of cooking water (see recipe, far left) for at least 4 hours before cooking. The easiest way to do this is to put it to soak in the morning, and cook it when you get home from work.

HOW TO CUT VEGETABLES

All vegetables for sushi rolls are ultimately cut into slender sticks.
Think of cutting most vegetables for sushi rolls into 2½-inch strips. A cucumber needs to be
cut in half lengthwise, then cut in half again, seeded, then cut lengthwise to form thin sticks.
Vegetables for other sushi, and for salads, need to be treated differently, but do take time
in their preparation, as a neat, attractive appearance is very important in Japanese food.

1 Cucumber cut for sushi rolls / **2** Avocado cut for sushi rolls / **3** Eggplant cut for nigiri (see page 46)
4 Daikon cut for salad (see page 83) / **5** Carrot cut for soup (see page 75)

HOW TO CHOOSE FISH

Most supermarkets now have fresh fish counters. Always pick up your fish from here rather than from the prepacked shelves, as being wrapped in plastic wrap can make the fish sweat. Whole fish can be easily filleted at the fish counter if you ask.

It's easy to spot fresh fish. The gills should be bright pink, not dark purple. The eyes should look clear and not gray or filmy.

Buying a whole salmon is not practical for home, so when choosing salmon fillet make sure it looks plump and firm. It's the same with tuna, which should be nice and red, not dark purple. When you cut it, the flesh should still look red, not silvery. If it smells too fishy or feels slimy, don't use it. Any fish used for sushi must be super-fresh; ask for "sushi grade."

I always rinse my fish in salty water and pat dry with strong paper towels before use. A lot of chefs don't bother, but I prefer to do this, as I feel it purifies and firms the flesh.

Try and buy fresh whole raw shrimp, which you can quickly cook yourself (see page 40). However, if you are in a rush, you can buy precooked shrimp. Always remove the black digestive tract, a string that runs down the back of the shrimp, and discard.

HOW TO CUT FISH FOR SUSHI

CUTTING TUNA FROM A BLOCK
1 Cut for sushi rolls / **2** Cut for sashimi / **3** Cut for nigiri (see overleaf for details)

HOW TO CUT FISH FOR SUSHI

TUNA

Start with a block of fresh tuna (ask the fishmonger for "sushi-grade"). It should be red with no discoloration, firm, and should not smell too fishy.

For sushi rolls, cut ½-inch sticks from the side of the block, against the grain of the fish as far as possible. Cut them into 2½- inch lengths before use.

For nigiri, cut thin diagonal slices, ¼ inch thick, working across the grain of the fish and using a long, stroking action. Each slice will show the grain.

For sashimi, cut slices vertically to the board, each about ½ inch thick, working across the grain of the fish. Make the slices as uniform as possible.

TO FILLET, SKIN, AND CUT WHOLE FISH

Using "sushi-grade" fish, stroke a slim, sharp, and flexible blade along one side of the spine. With the knife flat, stroke the blade over the bones to release the fillet. Turn and repeat.

Lay a fillet skin-down. Insert a knife between skin and flesh at one end, grab the skin with your free hand, angle the blade to the counter, and push it to the end of the fillet. For

sashimi, cut slices vertically to the board, about ½ inch thick. The slices should look pearly and display the attractive pattern of the grain.

For nigiri, cut thin diagonal slices, ¼ inch thick, working across the grain of the fish and using a long, stroking action. Each of the slices will show the grain.

SALMON

When choosing salmon fillets, go for "sushi-grade" that are bright, with no discoloration, and a good, thick size for sushi. Cut in half lengthwise.

The thinner part of the fillet is more suitable for sushi rolls. The more widely spaced grain of the thicker part is better for nigiri and sashimi.

Leave the thick part for cutting into ¼-inch slices on the diagonal for nigiri, and vertical ½-inch slices for sashimi (both cut as for tuna, see left).

Cut the thinner part into ½-inch sticks for sushi rolls. Be as even as possible. When you come to use them, cut them into roughly 2½-inch sections.

MACKEREL OR ANY COOKED OR CURED FISH

Mackerel is tasty and very healthy, but must be spanking fresh. Peel off the parchment-like skin with your fingers, as it can harbor bacteria.

A piece of Marinated Mackerel (see page 59) will look different to raw fish, being opaque. It is flaky, so hard to cut; you'll need your sharpest knife.

For nigiri or sashimi, start at the tail end of the fillet and cut very thin slices on the diagonal, holding the fish with your free hand to prevent it flaking away.

Turn the slices as you cut them, and lay them out on the board. Despite it having been skinned, mackerel slices will retain an attractive pattern.

SECRETS OF A JAPANESE PANTRY

A one-stop trip to a Japanese store can stock your kitchen pantry with authentic Japanese goodies. These have a long shelf life and can be relied upon to add amazing flavor in seconds.

1

NORI SEAWEED SHEETS
Essential for rolling sushi, these sheets of shredded, dried seaweed have a pleasing crispness and a neutral, slightly seaside flavor.

2

WASABI PASTE
The ubiquitous, eye-watering sushi accompaniment, this paste is made from a root not dissimilar to Western horseradish. Make sure yours is not too bright green nor too cheap, as there are fakes on the market.

3

WAKAME SEAWEED
Another edible seaweed, this is usually sold dried and shredded. It is great in salad (see page 89), or used as a topping for gunkan (see page 66).

4

SEASONED RICE VINEGAR
A sweetened vinegar used mostly to season sushi rice. This is worth buying as it is more convenient than making your own seasoning mixture from scratch.

5

SAKE
A dry rice wine, those you find in supermarkets and grocery stores (such as in the green bottle in the photo, left) are only good for cooking.

6

DRIED SOBA (BUCKWHEAT) NOODLES
These cook in minutes so they are great pantry ingredients, and perfect if you need a quick meal. They also make a great salad (see page 87).

7

JAPANESE SHORT-GRAIN RICE
Look for this in larger supermarkets. It is often labeled "sushi rice" and stores for ages. Brown sushi rice is not as common as white, but is worth seeking out when you Sushi Slim, as it will keep you feeling full for longer.

8

SESAME OIL
With a distinctive nutty taste, this oil is a wonderful accent for foods. Do not cook with it over a high heat, or its flavor will dissipate.

9

DASHI or **BONITO FLAKES**
These fish flakes are everywhere in Japanese cuisine. They provide a savory note to soups, omelets, stocks, and salad dressings.

10

SUSHI ROLLING MATS
Essential for rolling hosomaki and inside-out rolls (see pages 29–39), these are also light and easy to store.

11

LIGHT SOY SAUCE
Made from fermented soybeans, this is one of the most essential tastes of Japanese foods, replacing salt in most recipes.

12

MISO PASTE
An unique flavor and increasingly popular in the West. This paste, made from fermented soybeans, is hugely versatile: add to dishes, or use to make a quick soup.

EAT SUSHI–FEEL GREAT

*Wasabi is known for
its detox qualities, so you can feel purified
as you enjoy its hot, spicy flavor.*

Quick and easy sushi

HOSOMAKI
Step-by-step: how to make hosomaki rolls

Salmon
Tuna and chive
Crab stick and lettuce
Canned tuna and scallion
Avocado and chili
Bacon and asparagus
Green bean and miso
Corned beef and corn

INSIDE-OUT ROLLS
Step-by-step: how to make inside-out rolls

Smoked salmon, wasabi cream cheese, and lemon
Tempura shrimp and avocado
Sesame shrimp
Spicy salmon
Tuna and cucumber
Salmon and avocado
Tofu and pickles
Lettuce and pickled ginger
Okra and sesame

HIGH ROLLER

*Wrap your sushi rolling mat in a layer of plastic
wrap to keep it spotlessly clean and hygienic,
changing the plastic wrap between different rolls.*

HOW TO MAKE HOSOMAKI ROLLS

Cucumber roll

½ sheet of nori seaweed (halved horizontally)
¾ cup prepared sushi rice (see page 20, about the size of 2 medium eggs)
2 thin cucumber sticks

223 kcal per roll (6 pieces)

Place the seaweed near the bottom of a sushi rolling mat, rough side up and shiny side down. Place the rice in the middle of the seaweed.

Spread it out gently with your fingers to form an even covering all over the seaweed, leaving a ½-inch strip empty at the top edge furthest from you.

Place the cucumber in a straight line, left to right, across the middle of the rice. You are now ready to roll.

Gently slide both thumbs under the mat and rest your middle fingers on the cucumber. Lift the edge of the mat and seaweed nearest to you over the cucumber.

Lift up the leading edge of the mat with your right hand, if you are right-handed. (Or simply reverse all the instructions.) Roll, with your left hand supporting the roll. Pull gently on the mat with your right hand.

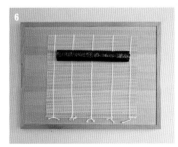

Gently squeeze the mat to form a tight roll. Remove the mat. With a very sharp knife, cut the roll in half. Put the halves together and cut into 6 pieces in total, wiping the blade between each cut.

A classic small roll, perfect for bite-size snacks, or popping into a bento box.

HOSOMAKI ROLLS

For each hosomaki roll (each roll makes 6 pieces), you will need:

½ sheet of nori seaweed (halved horizontally)
¾ cup prepared sushi rice (see page 20)

To make the hosomaki rolls, refer to the step-by-step guide (see page 31).

SALMON

2 salmon strips (see page 25)

281 kcal per roll (6 pieces)

TUNA AND CHIVE

2 tuna strips (see page 24)
5–6 chives, cut into 2½-inch lengths

256 kcal per roll (6 pieces)

CRAB STICK AND LETTUCE

2 crab sticks
1 teaspoon cream cheese
2 lettuce leaves

256 kcal per roll (6 pieces)

CANNED TUNA AND SCALLION

2 tablespoons canned tuna in brine,
drained
1 shredded scallion

243 kcal per roll (6 pieces)

AVOCADO AND CHILI

2 avocado slices
½ teaspoon chili powder (ideally
Japanese chili powder)

300 kcal per roll (6 pieces)

BACON AND ASPARAGUS

2 slices of broiled Canadian bacon
4 asparagus spears, blanched in salted water
for 3 minutes

310 kcal per roll (6 pieces)

GREEN BEAN AND MISO

6 green beans, blanched in salted water for 3
minutes
1 teaspoon miso paste

240 kcal per roll (6 pieces)

CORNED BEEF AND CORN

2 tablespoons canned corned beef
2 teaspoons corn kernels

260 kcal per roll (6 pieces)

HOW TO MAKE INSIDE-OUT ROLLS

Salmon and avocado roll

½ sheet of nori seaweed (halved horizontally)
1 cup prepared sushi rice (see page 20, about the size of a medium avocado)
1 teaspoon black sesame seeds
2 salmon strips (see page 25)
2 avocado slices

408 kcal per roll (6 pieces)

Place the seaweed near the bottom of a sushi rolling mat, rough side up and shiny side down. Place the sushi rice in the middle of the seaweed.

Spread the rice out gently with your fingers to form an even covering all over the seaweed. Press on the sesame seeds, or other coverings, so they stick.

Carefully turn over the whole piece, rice and seaweed, so the seaweed is on top. Add the salmon and avocado slices, or other fillings, across the middle.

Gently slide both thumbs under the mat and rest your middle fingers on the filling. Lift the edge of the mat and seaweed nearest to you over the filling.

Lift up the leading edge of the mat with your right hand, if you are right-handed. (Or simply reverse all the instructions.) Roll, with your left hand supporting the roll. Pull gently on the mat with your right hand.

Gently squeeze the mat to form a tight roll. Remove the mat. With a very sharp knife, cut the roll in half. Put the halves together and cut into 6 pieces in total, wiping the blade between each cut.

This American version of sushi is bright and colorful. My recipes ditch the heavy use of mayo and cream cheese in commercial inside-out rolls, but add more creaminess with avocado and a touch of cream cheese, if you like (though you'll increase the calories).

INSIDE-OUT ROLLS

For each inside-out roll (each roll makes 6 pieces), you will need:

½ sheet of nori seaweed
1 cup prepared sushi rice

To make the inside-out rolls, refer to the step-by-step guide (see left).

SMOKED SALMON, WASABI CREAM CHEESE, AND LEMON

For the covering
1½ ounces smoked salmon slices
6 very fine slices of unwaxed lemon

For the filling
1 tablespoon wasabi cream cheese
¾ ounce smoked salmon slices, cut into slim lengths

422 kcal per roll (6 pieces)

TEMPURA SHRIMP AND AVOCADO

For the covering
2 teaspoons tobiko (flying fish roe)
½ teaspoon black and white sesame seeds

For the filling
2 pieces King Shrimp Tempura (see page 40)
2 avocado slices
½ teaspoon shredded scallion

460 kcal per roll (6 pieces)

SESAME SHRIMP

For the covering
4 cooked, peeled and deveined shrimp (see page 40)
½ teaspoon black and white sesame seeds

For the filling
2 thin cucumber sticks
2 avocado slices

355 kcal per roll (6 pieces)

SPICY SALMON

For the covering
1½ ounces minced salmon
1 teaspoon chili powder (ideally
Japanese chili powder)
1½ teaspoons mayonnaise

For the filling
2 avocado slices
2 thin cucumber sticks

Simply mix the covering ingredients.

452 kcal per roll (6 pieces)

TUNA AND CUCUMBER

For the covering
½ teaspoon black and white sesame
seeds

For the filling
2 tuna strips (see page 24)
2 thin cucumber sticks

335 kcal per roll (6 pieces)

SALMON AND AVOCADO

For the covering
2 tablespoons tobiko (flying fish roe)

For the filling
2 salmon strips (see page 25)
2 avocado slices

400 kcal per roll (6 pieces)

TOFU AND PICKLES

For the covering
3 shiso leaves (or arugula leaves)

For the filling
1 tablespoon Japanese pickle
½ ounce tofu, cut into strips

288 kcal per roll (6 pieces)

LETTUCE AND PICKLED GINGER

For the filling
¼ ounce lettuce leaves
1 tablespoon pickled ginger

284 kcal per roll (6 pieces)

OKRA PODS AND SESAME

For the covering
½ teaspoon black and white sesame
seeds

For the filling
2–3 okra pods, blanched in salted
water for 2 minutes

295 kcal per roll (6 pieces)

Shrimp for sushi

HOW TO COOK SHRIMP FOR NIGIRI

Start with shell-on king shrimp. Insert a slim bamboo skewer into each, from underneath the tail, running up the belly to the head end. The idea is that the skewer keeps the shrimp straight.

Bring a large pan of salted water to a boil and add the shrimp on their skewers. Return to a boil and cook for 1 minute, or until completely pink, then drain and leave for 10 minutes.

Peel the shrimp and discard the shell and head, but leave the tail in place. Score the flesh of each shrimp up the belly, and open it out like a book.

Soak the shrimp in sushi rice seasoning vinegar, turning to coat all sides. Like this, covered, they can be kept in the refrigerator for 2 to 3 days. Blot the shrimp dry before use.

9 kcal per shrimp

KING SHRIMP TEMPURA

For the batter
¾ cup self-rising flour
3 tablespoons cornstarch
½ tablespoon baking powder
½ teaspoon salt

For the tempura
vegetable oil, to deep-fry
(about 4 cups)
12 raw king shrimp, deveined, tail left on

For the tempura sauce
scant ¼ cup light soy sauce
scant ¼ cup mirin
1 teaspoon bonito flakes

Sift all the ingredients for the batter into a bowl and pour in ⅔ cup of cold water, whisking to combine. Heat the oil to 350°F in a deep pan (you will need an oil thermometer to check the temperature).

Coat the shrimp in the batter, then drop into the oil for 3 minutes. Do not crowd the pan; cook in batches if necessary. Remove with a slotted spoon and drain on paper towels.

Meanwhile, for the sauce, put all the ingredients in a pan, pour in ¾ cup of water and bring to a boil. Serve warm with the tempura.

Serves 2
354 kcal per serving, **708 kcal** in total

Although we use batter, the Japanese version is much lighter than a Western one. Tempura sauce just gives the dish that extra treat factor. Feel free to substitute the shrimp with slices of sweet potato, carrot, eggplant, or broccoli, for a vegetarian version.

Nigiri

The original sushi

SMOOTH CUSTOMER

*Rub oil into your palms and fingers when making
nigiri, so the sushi rice won't stick. Use a
neutral-tasting oil, and avoid olive or sesame oil.*

HOW TO MAKE NIGIRI

Shrimp

trace of grapeseed oil or mayonnaise
1 tablespoon prepared sushi rice (see page 20, about the size of a medium cherry)
1 cooked shrimp (see page 40)

45 kcal per piece

Rub the grapeseed oil or mayonnaise into your palms and fingers. **Take the rice in your right hand, if you are right-handed. (Or simply reverse all the instructions.) Hold the shrimp (or other topping) in your left hand, across the base of your fingers.**

Place the rice on top of the fish. Put your right index finger on top of the rice. Wrap your left hand around your right index finger, squeezing gently to make a nice shape. Turn your nigiri so the fish is on top, still placed over the base of the fingers.

Repeat the wrapping and squeezing steps to form a neat, compact piece of nigiri. Do not squash the rice together too hard; all your movements should be gentle.

Now smooth the edges of the shrimp or other topping into an organic, graceful curve, with no corners: the topping should drape elegantly over the rice.

These are the favorite sushi in Japan, and were the first type. They are dainty and bite-size. Each recipe below makes 1 piece, simply scale up to make as many as you want.

NIGIRI

For each piece of nigiri, you will need:

trace of grapeseed oil or mayonnaise
1 tablespoon prepared sushi rice (see page 20, the size of a medium cherry)

To make the nigiri, refer to the step-by-step guide (see page 43).

TUNA

½ ounce tuna, sliced for nigiri (see page 24), for each piece

42 kcal per piece

SALMON

½ ounce salmon, sliced for nigiri (see page 25), for each piece

55 kcal per piece

SEA BREAM

½ ounce sea bream, sliced for nigiri (see page 24), for each piece

40 kcal per piece

SHRIMP

1 cooked shrimp (see page 40), for each piece

45 kcal per piece

BROILED ASPARAGUS

2 asparagus spears, broiled for 3 minutes on each side, for each piece
½-inch-thick strips of nori seaweed, for holding the asparagus in place

29 kcal per piece

EGGPLANT

¼ ounce Japanese eggplant slice, broiled for 3 minutes on each side, for each piece
sprinkling of finely grated gingerroot
scattering of very finely chopped scallion

Gently press the ginger and scallion on to the rice, then add the eggplant slice.

28 kcal per piece

AVOCADO

4 thin slices avocado, for each piece

53 kcal per piece

OKRA PODS AND SALTED PLUM

okra, blanched in salted water for
2 minutes, then halved, ½ for each piece
tiny cubes of Japanese salted plum

33 kcal per piece

Social sushi

HAND ROLLS
Step-by-step: how to make hand rolls

Make a wish
Monk roll
Fig surprise
Hint of lime
New York dream
Suzu yellowtail
Shrimp heaven
Omega-3 hit

GUNKAN
Step-by-step: how to make gunkan

Red and yellow bell pepper, onion, and mushroom
Shrimp, wasabi, and cream cheese
Butter grilled scallop
Seaweed, onion, and sesame soy sauce
Spicy salmon
Marinated tuna

PARTY PIECES

Anyone can roll a delicious, satisfying hand roll,
or fill a wonderful gunkan. So invite all your
friends and have a ball!

Sushi parties

This chapter contains the secrets to some of the best and
most memorable dinner parties you will ever throw.
Two types of sushi—gunkan (sushi "battleships"), and
hand rolls—are ideal for novices to make. Simply make
the sushi rice in advance (see page 20) and, in the case
of gunkan, make up a few gunkan bases (see page 64),
then lay out a cornucopia of filling ingredients on the table.
With just a few simple verbal tips, you can get everyone
around the table filling and rolling their own sushi, with
their own individual and unexpected combinations ...
perhaps you'll discover a future classic!

HOW TO MAKE HAND ROLLS

Salmon and avocado

½ sheet of nori seaweed (halved horizontally)
⅓ cup prepared sushi rice (see page 20, about the size of a medium egg)
2 thin cucumber sticks
2 salmon strips (see page 25)

157 kcal per roll

Place the seaweed on a counter, rough side up and shiny side down.

Take the rice and spread it on the left-hand side of the seaweed, if you are right-handed. (Or simply reverse all the instructions.)

Place the cucumber and salmon diagonally across the middle of the rice, so that they stick out at the top left corner. Pick up the rice-laden sheet of nori in your left hand.

Lift the bottom left corner of the seaweed up over the fillings to make a cone, then lift the right hand side of the seaweed and keep rolling. The nori sheet will stick to itself to seal the roll.

I call these the DIY rolls because you don't need any kit to make them. Each recipe below makes 1 roll, simply scale up to make as many as you want.

HAND ROLLS

For each hand roll, you will need:
½ sheet of nori seaweed (halved horizontally)
⅓ cup prepared sushi rice (see page 20, the size of a medium egg)

To make the hand roll, refer to the step-by-step guide (see page 55).

MAKE A WISH

3 okra pods, blanched in salted water for 2 minutes
pinch of shredded scallion
½ teaspoon black sesame seeds (optional)
4 shiso leaves (or see note overleaf)*

134 kcal per roll

MONK ROLL

1½ tablespoons grated carrot
1 shiso leaf (or see note overleaf)*
4 chives, cut into 2½-inch lengths
1 teaspoon black sesame seeds

128 kcal per roll

FIG SURPRISE

½ fresh fig, very thinly sliced
1 teaspoon cream cheese
3 very thin slices of unwaxed lemon

140 kcal per roll

HINT OF LIME

1 king scallop, sliced into 5 horizontally
3 very thin slices of organic lime

136 kcal per roll

NEW YORK DREAM

1½ tablespoon cream cheese mixed with ½ teaspoon
wasabi paste (wasabi cream cheese)
¾ ounce smoked salmon slices
2 very thin slices of unwaxed lemon
4 chives, cut into 2½-inch lengths
sprinkling of black and white sesame seeds

217 kcal per roll

SUZU YELLOWTAIL

1¼ ounce yellowtail, thinly sliced as for nigiri
(see page 24)
1 shiso leaf (or see note right)*
½ teaspoon black sesame seeds (optional)

202 kcal per roll

* If you can't find shiso leaves, substitute with a few chives and arugula leaves.

HOW TO MARINATE MACKEREL FOR SUSHI

Take as many spankingly fresh mackerel fillets as you need and peel off the parchment-like skin (see page 25). Salt on all sides and leave for 30 minutes.

Rinse off the salt. Place in a shallow non-reactive dish and add rice vinegar to soak, turning to coat the fillets on all sides. Cover and refrigerate overnight. The vinegar will 'cook' the fish. Pat dry to use.

SHRIMP HEAVEN

1 piece King Shrimp Tempura (see page 40)
3 avocado slices
1 teaspoon tobiko (flying fish roe, optional)

175 kcal per roll

OMEGA-3 HIT

1¼ ounces thinly sliced Marinated Mackerel (see above)
4 thin cucumber sticks

223 kcal per roll

HOW TO MAKE GUNKAN

Chopped shrimp

5 by 1¼-inch strips of nori seaweed
2 teaspoons prepared sushi rice (see page 20, about the size of a thumb)
2 shrimp, chopped

33 kcal per piece

Place the seaweed on a counter, rough side up and shiny side down.

Wrap the strip of seaweed around the rice, so the rough side faces inward. The rice should come just halfway up the seaweed case.

Gently press both ends of the seaweed strip together. They should stick to each other to seal. This is the gunkan base.

Fill the case with your chosen topping (in this case chopped shrimp), and serve.

Gunkan means "shape of the boat." They make a really pretty display. Each recipe below makes 5 pieces, simply scale up to make as many as you want.

GUNKAN

For each piece of gunkan, you will need:

5 by 1¼-inch strips of nori seaweed
2 teaspoons prepared sushi rice (the size of a thumb)

To make the gunkan, refer to the step-by-step guide (see left).

RED AND YELLOW BELL PEPPER, ONION, AND MUSHROOM

1 teaspoon vegetable oil
½ yellow bell pepper, cut into ¼-inch cubes
½ red bell pepper, cut into ¼-inch cubes
½ small onion, cut into ¼-inch cubes
4 small mushroom, cut into ¼-inch cubes

Place a pan over medium heat and add the oil. Add all the vegetables and cook for 5 minutes. Cool down for 10 minutes.

Divide between the gunkan.

48 kcal per piece

SHRIMP, WASABI, AND CREAM CHEESE

2 ounces cooked shrimp (see page 40), chopped
⅔ cup cream cheese
2 tablespoons wasabi
a few scallions pieces, very finely chopped, to serve (optional)

In a small bowl, mix the shrimp well with the cream cheese and wasabi, cover, and leave in the refrigerator for 30 minutes.

Divide between the gunkan and top with the scallion slivers (if using) to serve.

153 kcal per piece

BUTTER GRILLED SCALLOP

2 teaspoons unsalted butter
2 ounces scallops, cut into ½-inch cubes
1 teaspoon soy sauce

Melt the butter in a small skillet over medium heat.

Add the scallops and cook for 3 minutes, until brown on all sides. Add the soy sauce, turn the scallops to coat, then remove from the skillet, cover, and marinate for 15 minutes.

Divide between the gunkan.

47 kcal per piece

SEAWEED, ONION, AND SESAME SOY SAUCE

4 tablespoons dried wakame seaweed
⅛ cup finely sliced onion
1 tablespoon soy sauce
1 teaspoon lemon juice
½ teaspoon white sesame seeds

Place the seaweed and onion in separate bowls, cover with cold water, and let soak for 15 minutes.

Drain the seaweed and squeeze the water out. Drain the onion and pat dry with paper towels. Mix the onion and seaweed in a bowl. Add the soy sauce, lemon juice, and sesame seeds and mix well.

Divide between the gunkan.

29 kcal per piece

SPICY SALMON

2 ounces salmon
½ teaspoon mayonnaise
1 teaspoon eel sauce (from Asian stores; this is sweet,
thick soy sauce)
½ teaspoon chili powder (ideally Japanese chili powder)

Mince the salmon with a sharp knife, place in a small bowl,
and add the mayonnaise, eel sauce, and chili. Mix well.

Divide between the gunkan.

47 kcal per piece

MARINATED TUNA

2 ounces tuna
1 teaspoon soy sauce
1 teaspoon mirin
pinch of minced scallion (optional)

Slice the tuna into ½-inch chunks, place in a small bowl,
and add the soy sauce and mirin. Stir, cover, and let
marinate for 15 minutes.

Divide between the gunkan. Sprinkle with the scallion
to serve (if using).

36 kcal per piece

Soups and salads

MISO
Tofu and seaweed
Hearty root vegetable
Eggplant
Mackerel
Spicy pork
Scallion and spinach
Potato and onion
Shiitake mushroom, spinach, and onion

SECRETS OF THE JAPANESE POWER BREAKFAST
Japanese omelet
Pickles
Broiled salmon

COLLAGEN SOUPS
Chicken collagen soup
Facelift-in-a-bowl

SALADS
Japanese coleslaw
Steamed vegetables with creamy tofu dressing
Oil-free mushroom salad
Lightly grilled tuna with arugula
Eggplant and shallot salad
Oil-free edamame
No-carb "wrap wrap wrap"
Fill-you-up soba noodle salad
Tuna and avocado tartare
Popeye spinach salad
Onion and seaweed salad
Steamed sesame chicken salad

MIGHTY MISO

Despite the fact that miso is a thin soup, and very low in calories, drinking it can fill you up disproportionately. Try having a cup with each meal.

Miso soup is a favorite of mine, as you can come up with so many varieties depending on what you have in your pantry or refrigerator. It's nutritious but calorie-light. Here are some of my most popular crowd-pleasers. If you are a vegetarian, simply use a miso paste that does not contain bonito flakes, and omit any other bonito flakes in the recipe.

TO MAKE BASIC MISO SOUP

2 teaspoons miso paste with
bonito flakes

Boil ⅔ cup of water in a pan, then
reduce the heat to low. Put the miso
paste on a spoon. Immerse half of the
spoon into the boiling water, mixing
the paste and a small amount of water
together on the spoon to form a roux.
Mix this roux into the rest of the water
in the pan.

Makes 1 bowl
30 kcal per bowl

TOFU AND SEAWEED

Pictured on page 73

1 teaspoon dried wakame seaweed
1 quantity Basic Miso Soup
¾ ounce firm tofu, cut into ½-inch cubes

Soak the seaweed in water for 10 minutes, then drain and add to the miso with the tofu.

Makes 1 bowl
46 kcal per bowl

HEARTY ROOT VEGETABLE

Pictured left

½ teaspoon bonito flakes
2 ounces daikon, finely sliced
1 small carrot, finely sliced
½ large onion, minced
1 tablespoon miso paste

Boil 2½ cups of water in a pan. Add the bonito flakes and all the vegetables. Cook them for 3 minutes, until the vegetables soften. Turn the heat off.

Add the miso paste to the soup through a small strainer, using a teaspoon to push it through.

Turn the heat back on until it boils, stirring, then serve.

Makes 2 bowls
59 kcal per bowl

EGGPLANT

1 slice Japanese eggplant
1 quantity Basic Miso Soup

Broil the eggplant for 3 minutes on each side, then cut into ½-inch cubes. Add to the miso.

Makes 1 bowl
34 kcal per bowl

MACKEREL

¾ ounce smoked mackerel, sliced
1 quantity Basic Miso Soup

Add the fish to the soup just long enough to heat through, then serve.

Makes 1 bowl
70 kcal per bowl

SPICY PORK

¾ ounce Spicy Miso Ground Meat with pork (see page 100)
1 quantity Basic Miso Soup

Add the pork to the soup just long enough to heat through, then serve.

Makes 1 bowl
100 kcal per bowl

SCALLION AND SPINACH

large pinch of shredded scallion
5 large spinach leaves
1 quantity Basic Miso Soup

Add the scallion and spinach to the miso just before serving.

Makes 1 bowl
33 kcal per bowl

POTATO AND ONION

1¼ ounce potato, cut into ½-inch cubes
2 teaspoons miso paste with bonito flakes
a few thin slices of onion

Cook the potato in ⅔ cup of boiling water until just tender, before adding the miso. Add the onion to serve.

Makes 1 bowl
55 kcal per bowl

SHIITAKE MUSHROOM, SPINACH, AND ONION

2–3 shiitake mushrooms, sliced
3 large spinach leaves
a few thin slices of onion
2 teaspoons miso paste with bonito

Place the mushrooms, spinach, and onion in ⅔ cup of boiling water for 3 minutes. Add the miso, then serve.

Makes 1 bowl
36 kcal per bowl

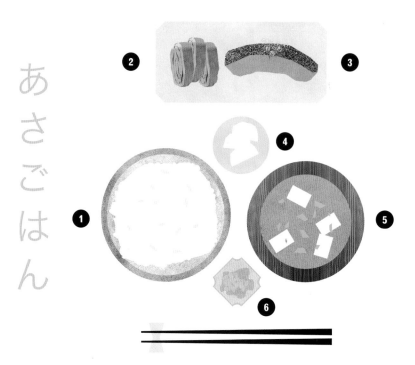

あさごはん

1 ½ cup cooked rice **168 kcal** / 2 1¼ ounces Japanese omelet **86 kcal** / 3 4 ounces broiled salmon **246 kcal**
4 ¾ ounce Japanese pickles **6 kcal** / 5 ½ cup miso soup **24 kcal** / 6 1 tablespoon natto **30 kcal**
560 kcal total

Secrets of the Japanese power breakfast

The traditional Japanese breakfast is a hearty feast, a world away from a slice of toast grabbed on the go. A spread of dishes charms the eye and satisfies the taste buds ... though the flavors are a little stronger than those Westerners are used to at breakfast.

If you have made, portioned, and frozen the rice and omelet parts of breakfast, and have a jar of Japanese pickles, it will only take five minutes to broil the salmon and make the soup.

You do not have to eat a Japanese breakfast to follow Sushi Slim, so this is here just to show you what you're missing! If you want to try it, but don't have time during the week, give it a go for brunch at the weekend. You will find that you'll struggle to eat later in the day ... which is, of course, part of the secret of the enviable Japanese figure.

Natto, a relish of fermented soybeans, can be an acquired taste. We mix it with soy sauce and eat it with rice. Try it; it's addictive.

When sugar is added to the omelet, it is usually used to top or fill sushi; whereas the sugar-free version is used in hot food. Obviously, children prefer the version with sugar!

A Japanese omelet is denser than the Western type and is cut into slices to be chilled for up to three days, or wrapped and frozen, or eaten straight away, as desired.

JAPANESE OMELET WITHOUT SUGAR

1½ teaspoons cornstarch
6 free-range eggs
1 teaspoon salt
1 tablespoon sesame oil (optional)

Slake the cornstarch in 7 tablespoons of water in a large bowl. Beat in the eggs with the salt.

Add the sesame oil to a skillet over medium heat. (If you use a nonstick skillet you won't need the oil.)

Add one ladle's worth of egg mixture to the pan, tilting it until the bottom is completely covered. Cook until the egg mixture is just about to set.

Fold the egg over on itself three times in 2½-inch folds. Keep the omelet in the pan, and ladle more egg into the newly made space, lifting the first omelet with a spatula to allow the raw egg to flow underneath.

Once the new egg mixture ia about to set, fold three times again, encasing the first omelet, creating a layered effect. Repeat until the egg mixture has been used up. Serve, or divide into 6, wrap, and freeze separately.

Serves 6
516 kcal in total, **86 kcal** per serving

JAPANESE OMELET WITH SUGAR

Make as above, but add to the egg mixture:

½ teaspoon bonito flakes, dissolved in a little water
1 teaspoon soy sauce
1½ tablespoons superfine sugar

Serves 6
872 kcal in total, **145 kcal** per serving

JAPANESE PICKLES

You can of course buy these pickles, but this is a very light, salty relish to add pep to your meals. It will store in the refrigerator for 3 to 5 days.

1¼–1½ pounds head of Chinese leaf or cabbage
1 tablespoon sea salt
1 dried chile
1 garlic clove, finely sliced

Cut the Chinese leaf into quarters and wash it well.

Put it into a nonreactive plastic container and add the salt, chile, and garlic. Mix well, then weight down with a sterilzed stone, or a plate with cans of food on top.

Leave for half a day before eating.

Makes enough for 5 family breakfasts
180–210 kcal in total

BROILED SALMON

One of the healthiest and most common breakfast dishes in Japan. Think of it as an alternative to kippers or kedgeree.

1 teaspoon sea salt
4 ounces salmon fillet

Sprinkle the salt on to all sides of the salmon and leave it for 20 minutes.

Broil it for 5 minutes, turning once.

Serve.

Serves 1
246 kcal

Beauty departments are now filled with sachets of liquid collagen to add to your beauty routine, but in Japan we incorporate this goodie into our daily diet. The skin-tightening effects are visible even the day after eating.

I give chicken and fish versions of Collagen Soup here and overleaf.

There is a restaurant in Tokyo that I have been to three times where they only serve collagen-rich grouper soup, in large communal bowls. The restaurant is full of women diners, who fight over the extra-rich soup left in the bottom of the bowl, while they are served by the all-male waiting staff.

We are taught that collagen is most easily absorbed by the body when it comes from fish, though it is also absorbed when it comes from poultry. Although red meat contains collagen, we think it is difficult to digest and so does not do the same great job on the skin.

CHICKEN COLLAGEN SOUP

3¼ pounds medium whole chicken
1 tablespoon sea salt
1¼-inch gingerroot, sliced, slices crushed with the back of a knife
1 leek, finely sliced lengthwise and cut into 2½-inch lengths
1 teaspoon black pepper

Pour 4 cups of water into a large pan and add the chicken, salt, and ginger. Bring to a boil over medium heat, then reduce the heat and simmer for 30 minutes.

Remove the chicken from the pan and remove all the bones and skin. Strain the stock, then return it to the rinsed-out pan. Return the chicken meat to the pan with the leek. Return to a gentle simmer, and cook for another 10 minutes.

Season with black pepper and serve in warmed soup bowls.

If not serving immediately, let cool thoroughly at room temperature in a shallow, sealed container, then chill in the refrigerator. Once it's chilled it takes on a jelly-like quality and you should be able to cut it into 3-inch cubes (see far left). Pop a couple of these into a flask or sealed cup and simply microwave for 2 minutes for a lunchtime super-beautifying soup. Store the rest in your freezer and use it up within 1 month.

If you like, you can add grated carrot and sliced shiitake mushroom caps to each bowl of soup.

You can also freeze the cubes without chicken meat for a far lower-calorie collagen soup.

Serves 4
1,196 kcal in total, with chicken meat
299 kcal per bowl, with chicken meat

Grouper is full of collagen and, for that reason, it is expensive in Japan and the food of the rich and famous. It is economical in the West, though.

You can of course omit the fish head, but you will lose a lot of collagen if you do. I promise you, it's worth it!

FACELIFT-IN-A-BOWL

1 grouper head, plus 3½–4-ounce grouper fillet
½ x 15-ounce package of firm tofu (optional)
½ leek
¾ ounce Chinese leaf, cut into ¾-inch strips
¼ cup bean sprouts
2 fresh shiitake mushrooms, cut into ½-inch slices
3 tablespoons soy sauce
½-inch gingerroot, grated
2-inch daikon, grated

Put the fish head and 2 cups of water in a large pan. Bring slowly to a boil, then reduce the heat, cover, and simmer for 15 minutes. Remove and discard the fish head. At this point, you may chill, or freeze, the soup base in cubes, as for Chicken Collagen Soup (see page 79). It will be extremely low in calories in this ungarnished state.

Cut the tofu (if using) into ¾-inch cubes. Cut the leek into 1¼-inch chunks, then cut these into lengthwise strips.

Return the fish stock to a boil, then add the grouper fillet, tofu, leek, Chinese leaf, bean sprouts, and shiitake mushrooms. Cover and cook over medium heat for 10 minutes.

Uncover and add the soy sauce, ginger, and daikon. Serve immediately in warmed bowls.

Serves 2
420 kcal in total
210 kcal per bowl

This Japanese coleslaw is mayo-free and very refreshing, with the low heat of the daikon adding a mild kick. Use bonito flakes instead of scallion if you eat fish.

We have become used to roasting vegetables. Steaming them is a much healthier option, and the tofu dressing adds a lush silkiness to this dish.

Western mushroom recipes sometimes taste heavy, as they absorb a lot of oil. This raw, no-oil salad is much lighter, but has a gorgeously dense bite to it.

JAPANESE COLESLAW

1 daikon radish
1 carrot
2 tablespoons soy sauce
2 tablespoons sesame oil
2 tablespoons rice vinegar
2 tablespoons mirin
1 teaspoon superfine sugar
1 tablespoon white sesame seeds, crushed in a mortar and pestle
3 tablespoons finely chopped scallion

Finely slice the daikon and carrot (or shred them using a mandolin), then rinse under cold water.

Mix together all the remaining ingredients, except the scallion, to make a dressing.

Place the vegetables in a bowl and toss with the dressing. Mound the daikon and carrot like a mountain on a large plate, sprinkle with the scallion, and it's ready!

Serves 2 as an accompaniment
450 kcal in total
225 kcal per serving

STEAMED VEGETABLES WITH CREAMY TOFU DRESSING

For the salad
1 red bell pepper
1 yellow bell pepper
¼ daikon radish
1 celery stalk
1 teaspoon sesame seeds

For the dressing
4 ounces silken tofu
10 chives
2 tablespoons light soy sauce
1 tablespoon lemon juice

Cut all the vegetables into bite-size pieces and steam for 3 minutes. Drain, then cool them down.

Mix all the ingredients for the dressing in the blender and mix it through the vegetables, then serve, sprinkled with the sesame seeds.

Serves 2
222 kcal in total
111 kcal per serving

OIL-FREE MUSHROOM SALAD

4 shiitake mushrooms
2 enoki mushrooms
2 oyster mushrooms
4 closed cup mushrooms
½ teaspoon sea salt

Cut the hard part of the stems from the shiitake mushrooms, then trim and finely slice all the mushrooms and sprinkle with sea salt.

Lay them all next to each other on a broiler pan and cook under a hot broiler for 5 minutes, turning to cook all sides.

Eat them as they are, or with Wasabi Dressing (see page 100).

Serves 2 as an accompaniment
15 kcal in total, without dressing
7.5 kcal per serving, without dressing

The Japanese version of a classic combination. I find the freshness of this dish incredibly cleansing and healthy feeling.

A funky raw food recipe, this tastes rich and will fill you up, but is full of fiber and nutrients.

A perfect 30-second fix to add to a bento box, or grab as a quick snack.

LIGHTLY GRILLED TUNA WITH ARUGULA
Pictured left

1 teaspoon sea salt
7 ounces sushi-grade tuna block
1 cup arugula salad
1 teaspoon black and white sesame seeds

For the sauce

2 tablespoons soy sauce
1 teaspoon superfine sugar
1½ tablespoons rice vinegar
1 teaspoon sesame oil

Sprinkle the salt on all sides of the tuna and leave it for 15 minutes.

Preheat a nonstick pan over the highest heat. When it is very hot, add the tuna. As soon as it colors, turn it to color on another side. Remove from the pan once it is seared all over. Place on a plate, cover, and put in the refrigerator to cool rapidly for 15 minutes.

Mix together all the ingredients for the sauce.

Slice the tuna into wafer-thin slices, place it on a plate with the arugula, drizzle with the sauce, and scatter with the sesame seeds, serving any remaining sauce on the side.

Serves 2
328 kcal in total
164 kcal per serving

EGGPLANT AND SHALLOT SALAD

1 (14 ounce) Japanese eggplant
2 tablespoons sea salt
4 shallots, finely sliced
1 tablespoon sesame oil
1 tablespoon light soy sauce
½ tablespoon lemon juice
1 teaspoon white sesame seeds, crushed in a mortar and pestle
5 chives, finely chopped

Cut the eggplant into ⅝-inch slices. Place in a bowl and sprinkle with the salt. Rub it through the slices for at least 3 minutes, then rinse and pat the slices dry with paper towels.

Place in a bowl and add the shallots, then sprinkle the other ingredients on top, toss, and serve.

Serves 2 as an accompaniment
312 kcal in total
156 kcal per serving

OIL-FREE EDAMAME

9 ounces frozen edamame beans
½ teaspoon sea salt

Defrost the beans, then sprinkle with the salt.

Serves 2 as an accompaniment
398 kcal in total
199 kcal per serving

An indulgent dish, but very low in carbohydrate. Without realizing it you will be eating a lot of greens here, while enjoying a heady hit of umami, the irresistible savory flavor.

NO CARB "WRAP WRAP WRAP"

9 ounces beef fillet

For the marinade
1 tablespoon soy sauce
thin wedge of eating apple, finely grated
½ teaspoon finely grated garlic
1 teaspoon finely grated gingerroot
½ tablespoon chili powder (ideally Japanese chili powder)
1 teaspoon English mustard powder
1 tablespoon sesame oil

For the salad
1 round lettuce, washed, leaves separated
¼ daikon radish, shredded
1 cucumber, sliced into thin sticks
2 garlic cloves, finely sliced

Put the beef in the freezer for 1 hour to firm up (but make sure you don't forget about it: you don't want it to freeze). This will make it easier to slice thinly. Slice the beef as thinly as you can.

Mix all the marinade ingredients in a bowl, add the beef, and mix well. Cover and let marinate for 20 minutes. Preheat a broiler. Broil the beef for 2 or 3 minutes on each side.

To assemble the wrap, hold a lettuce leaf in your hand, add some daikon and cucumber, then some beef and garlic. Wrap the lettuce leaf around and eat.

Serves 2
566 kcal in total
283 kcal per serving

A great recipe to keep hunger at bay, light, but incredibly tasty. I find this salad quite addictive. You can make more noodles than you need, then wrap portions individually and freeze them. Defrost under running water. Don't be tempted to defrost them in a microwave, as this will soften their texture.

FILL-YOU-UP SOBA NOODLE SALAD

For the salad
7 ounces soba noodles
1 cup baby spinach leaves
handful of cherry tomatoes (optional)

For the dressing
4 tablespoons sesame oil
6 tablespoons soy sauce
2 tablespoons lemon juice
2 tablespoons white sesame seeds, crushed in a mortar and pestle, plus more to serve
2 teaspoons chili powder (ideally Japanese chili powder)

Bring 3½ quarts of water to a boil and cook the soba noodles for 15 minutes (or according to the package directions). Drain, then rinse the noodles under cold water. Drain really well once more.

Mix together all the ingredients for the dressing.

Put the noodles, spinach, and tomatoes (if using) in a bowl, toss with the dressing, sprinkle with sesame seeds, and serve.

Serves 2
1,002 kcal in total
501 kcal per serving

A tuna dish with an incredibly luxurious texture, this is a really healthy but indulgent treat.

Spinach and sesame salad is a must-eat in Japan. We keep it in the refrigerator to eat daily.

This is incredibly refreshing and clean tasting. I would eat it every day if I could.

TUNA AND AVOCADO TARTARE

For the onion dressing
1 onion, roughly chopped
1 tablespoon clear honey
1 tablespoon sushi vinegar
1 tablespoon grapeseed oil
¼ teaspoon sea salt
¼ teaspoon black pepper
½ tablespoon dill, minced

For the tartare
2 ounces sushi-grade tuna loin
½ avocado

Blitz all the ingredients for the onion dressing in a blender until smooth.

With a sharp knife, finely mince the tuna. Now you can go 2 ways: either slice the avocado and place the slices on a mound of tuna, or mash the avocado to a smooth paste and mix it in with the minced tuna.

Serve it with the onion dressing, and with wasabi paste for dipping.

Serves 2
456 kcal in total
228 kcal per serving

POPEYE SPINACH SALAD

9 ounces frozen spinach
½ tablespoon white sesame seeds, crushed in a mortar and pestle
½ tablespoon soy sauce
1 teaspoon superfine sugar
½ tablespoon sesame oil

Put the spinach in a pan and add just enough water to cover. Bring to a boil, reduce the heat, and simmer until the spinach has defrosted. Drain and, when cool enough to handle, squeeze out all the water.

Put the spinach in a bowl and mix in the remaining ingredients. Toss and serve.

Serves 2 as an accompaniment
184 kcal in total
92 kcal per serving

ONION AND SEAWEED SALAD

2 tablespoons dried wakame seaweed
1 onion, finely sliced
2 tablespoons lemon juice
1 tablespoon light soy sauce
1 tablespoon mirin

Soak the seaweed and onion separately in water for 15 minutes, then drain. Squeeze the excess water from the seaweed, and pat the onion dry on paper towels. Place both into a bowl.

Add the lemon juice, soy sauce, and mirin and mix well.

Serves 2 as an accompaniment
138 kcal in total
69 kcal per serving

This is my family's favorite salad; it's filling, tasty, but incredibly healthy.

STEAMED SESAME CHICKEN SALAD

For the dressing
4 tablespoons soy sauce
4 tablespoons superfine sugar
3 tablespoons rice vinegar
½ cube chicken bouillon
½ teaspoon sea salt
1 tablespoon sesame oil

For the salad
1 teaspoon sea salt
1 chicken breast
2 tablespoons sake
½ medium Iceberg lettuce, thinly sliced
½ cucumber, thinly sliced
a few wedges of tomato
a few thin slices of red onion

Put everything for the dressing except the sesame oil into a pan with 8 tablespoons of water. Place over low heat and bring to a boil. Stir, making sure both the sugar and chicken bouillon cube completely dissolve. Remove from the heat, let cool, then add the sesame oil, cover, and chill until needed.

Sprinkle the salt on the chicken on both sides and place on a heatproof dish. Add the sake.

Put ¾ inch of cold water in a large pan and add a trivet that emerges above the level of the water. Place the chicken dish on the trivet. Cover the pan.

Place the pan on the stove and cook on medium heat for 25 minutes from start to finish.

Remove the dish from the pan, and leave until cool enough to handle. Tear the chicken into strips.

Put the lettuce on a plate and arrange the cucumber, tomato, and red onion over. Put the chicken on top. Toss with the sesame dressing and serve.

Serves 2
494 kcal in total
247 kcal per serving

Beautiful bentos
The ultimate lunch box

NO. 1
Mighty meat

NO. 2
Stuffed bell peppers and rice balls

NO. 3
Chicken teriyaki

NO. 4
Low-fat protein punch

NO. 5
Sweet chili shrimp

NO. 6
Spicy chicken-and-egg

NO. 7
Inside-out rolls

NO. 8
Salad day

NO. 9
Omega-3 and wasabi veg

NO. 10
Inside-out rolls with protein boost

MAKE YOUR BOSS JEALOUS!

All the constituent parts of each bento can be made at the weekend, wrapped, and frozen in portions. Aim for lots of different colors in a bento, for maximum nutrition.

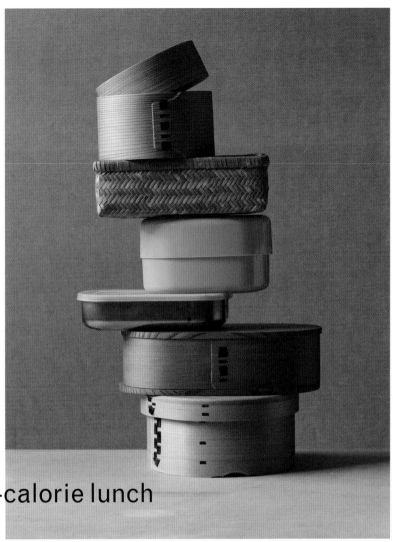

The 500-calorie lunch

Lunch can be a dangerous time when you are watching what you eat. But what if you could take to work a feast; a whole panoply of delicious dishes wrapped up in a beautiful box, safe in the knowledge that someone else has counted the calories for you? Well, now you can.

Here are 10 bento boxes, one for every working day of two weeks, each of which contains around 500 calories. Every recipe can be made in a trice at the weekend, wrapped, and frozen in portions. On a working morning, it's simply a case of packing your selection

of dishes from the freezer. By lunch time, your food will be perfectly defrosted. You can mix and match the components of the bento boxes that follow, just bear in mind that this may tip the calorie count to more than 500.

You'll be the envy of your workmates, eating a healthier, more satisfying option than a mayo-laden sandwich. I tend to follow a rough rule of one-half rice, one-quarter vegetables, and one-quarter protein in a bento box, and you can include Miso or Collagen Soups (see pages 74–75 and 78–81) in winter.

キレイなお弁当

NO. 1
Mighty meat

TOFU STEAK
SPICY MISO GROUND MEAT
MIXED SEAWEED WITH
OKRA PODS
WHITE RICE

507 kcal

NO. 2
Stuffed bell peppers and rice balls

STUFFED GREEN BELL PEPPERS
WITH TURKEY ONIGIRI
BROILED PUMPKIN
FRESH TOMATOES

501 kcal

NO. 3
Chicken teriyaki

CHICKEN TERIYAKI
EDAMAME RICE
GREEN BEANS AND
ALMOND BUTTER
CREAMY PUMPKIN

495 kcal

NO. 4
Low-fat protein punch

BROILED SALMON
JAPANESE OMELET
WITH CHIVES
OIL-FREE MUSHROOM SALAD
POPEYE SPINACH SALAD
BROWN RICE

509 kcal

NO. 5
Sweet chili shrimp

SWEET CHILI SHRIMP
JAPANESE OMELET WITH
EDAMAME OR GREEN PEA
ASPARAGUS WITH
MUSHROOMS AND SESAME OIL
BROWN RICE

500 kcal

キレイなお弁当

NO. 6
Spicy chicken-and-egg

**SPICY CHICKEN
BOILED ASPARAGUS
BALSAMIC PICKLED EGG
BROWN RICE**

504 kcal

NO. 7
Inside-out rolls

**JAPANESE OMELET, BEAN, AND
CRAB INSIDE-OUT ROLL
OIL-FREE EDAMAME**

482 kcal

NO. 8
Salad day

**FILL-YOU-UP SOBA NOODLE
SALAD**

501 kcal

NO. 9
Omega-3 and wasabi veg

**SMOKED MACKEREL
JAPANESE OMELET WITH
EDAMAME OR GREEN PEA
MIXED VEGETABLES WITH
WASABI DRESSING
WHITE RICE**

459 kcal

NO. 10
Inside-out rolls with protein boost

**SMOKED SALMON AND
CUCUMBER INSIDE-OUT ROLL
JAPANESE OMELET
OIL-FREE EDAMAME**

489 kcal

NO. 1
Mighty meat

For days when you fancy a bit more protein.

TOFU STEAK

If you are craving a meaty texture, switch to this dish. It's bursting with vegetable proteins that are easy to digest.

For the tofu steak
1 pound 4 ounces firm tofu
1 teaspoon sea salt
1 teaspoon finely grated gingerroot
3 tablespoons cornstarch
5 tablespoons cooking oil

For the wasabi dressing
2 tablespoons soy sauce
½ tablespoon wasabi paste
1 teaspoon grapeseed oil

Place a few layers of paper towels on a plate. Remove the tofu from the package and put it on the paper towels. Leave for 20 minutes, to remove all the moisture. Cut into 1¼-inch squares and place in a bowl. Add the sea salt and ginger and sprinkle with the cornstarch. Turn to coat on all sides.

Heat a pan over medium heat and add the cooking oil. Add the tofu to the pan and brown on all sides.

Meanwhile, mix all the ingredients for the dressing in a small bowl. Mix the tofu steaks with the wasabi dressing and serve. Or divide into 8 portions, wrap, and freeze separately. Use 1 portion for a bento box.

Makes 8 bento box portions
1,056 kcal in total
132 kcal per serving

SPICY MISO GROUND MEAT

An Asian twist on a ground dish.

¾ tablespoon cooking oil
1 cup minced scallion
2 teaspoons finely grated gingerroot
2 teaspoons minced garlic
9 ounces ground pork or turkey
1¼ tablespoons superfine sugar
1¾ tablespoons miso paste
3 tablespoons soy sauce
2½ tablespoons sake
¾ chicken bouillon cube
1¼ teaspoon tobanjan (chili bean sauce, optional)

Heat the oil in a skillet over low heat. Add the scallion, ginger, and garlic and stir well until softened.

Add the ground meat, increase the heat to medium., and cook until lightly brown. Add all the other ingredients except the tobanjan with 2 tablespoons of water, stir, and cook for 5 minutes, or until all the liquid has evaporated.

Add the tobanjan (if using), and serve. Or divide into 4 portions, wrap, and freeze separately. Use 1 portion for a bento box.

Makes 4 bento box portions
with turkey **536 kcal** in total;
with pork **928 kcal** in total
with turkey **134 kcal** per serving;
with pork **232** per serving

MIXED SEAWEED WITH OKRA PODS

Bursting with vitamins and minerals that all add beauty and health benefits to this gorgeous side dish.

8 okra pods
½ teaspoon salt
8 tablespoons mixed edible seaweed
4 tablespoons soy sauce

4 tablespoons lime juice

Add the okra pods and salt to boiling water for 1 minute. Drain, and chop finely. Put the seaweed in a bowl, cover with warm water, and soak for 10 minutes. Drain and squeeze out the water.

Mix the okra pods, seaweed, soy sauce, and lime juice. Serve, or divide into 4 portions, wrap, and freeze separately. Use 1 portion for a bento box.

Makes 4 bento box portions
108 kcal in total
27 kcal per serving

WHITE RICE

Add 1 cup cooked Japanese white rice (see page 20) to this bento box.

Makes 1 bento box portion
214 kcal per serving

NO. 2
Stuffed bell peppers and rice balls

Simple to prepare, but very impressive!

STUFFED GREEN BELL PEPPERS WITH TURKEY

Make extra of this at supper for tomorrow's bento box. Delicious.

1¼ cups minced onion
1 teaspoon cooking oil, for the onion, plus 1 tablespoon for the peppers
17 ounces ground turkey
salt, to taste
1 egg, beaten

4 small green bell peppers
4 teaspoons all-purpose flour
4 tablespoons balsamic vinegar
2 tablespoons mirin

Cook the onion over medium heat with the 1 teaspoon of oil until soft. Tip into a bowl. Add the turkey, salt, and egg and mix well. Leave for 20 minutes.

Cut each bell pepper in half and remove the seeds and ribs. Fill each half with the turkey mixture, and sprinkle the turkey with the flour.

Add the 1 tablespoon of oil to a skillet over medium heat. Add the bell peppers, turkey-side down. Cook for 3 minutes. Turn and cook for another 3 minutes.

Add the balsamic vinegar and mirin, cover, and cook for a final 5 minutes, or until the bell pepper has softened and the stuffing is cooked through. Serve, or divide into 4 portions, wrap, and freeze separately. Use 1 portion for a bento box.

Makes 4 bento box portions
1,146 kcal in total
287 kcal per serving

ONIGIRI

Traditional Japanese rice balls are an easy low-calorie lunch time snack, great for when you need a carb hit.

2¼ cups hot, cooked Japanese white rice (see page 20)
salt
4 thick strips of nori seaweed

Take one-quarter of the rice and mold it into a ball in your hands.

Sprinkle salt all over the rice and pat it in firmly, then wrap the seaweed around the rice and it's ready to eat! Repeat to use all the rice and

seaweed. If making in advance, wrap and freeze each onigiri separately. Use 1 onigiri in a bento box.

Makes 4 bento box portions
683 kcal in total
171 kcal per serving

BROILED PUMPKIN

Couldn't be simpler. Broiling gives pumpkin a real sweetness for when you need a sugary-but-healthy fix.

1 small pumpkin or acorn squash
salt

Cut the pumpkin into ¼-inch-thick slices. Lay them on a broiler pan and cook under a hot broiler for 5 minutes, turning to cook both sides. You should get speckles of black.

Sprinkle salt all over the pumpkin. Serve, or divide into 4 portions, wrap, and freeze separately. Use 1 portion for a bento box.

Makes 4 bento box portions
116 kcal in total
29 kcal per serving

FRESH TOMATOES

Add 3 fresh cherry tomatoes to each bento box.

14 kcal per serving

Most Westerners know this dish. Popular the world over for its sweet-salty tastiness, it contains plenty of garlic and ginger.

CHICKEN TERIYAKI

4 skinless chicken breasts
(each 3½ ounces)
4 teaspoons vegetable oil

For the sauce
2 tablespoons soy sauce
4 teaspoons mirin
2 tablespoons sake
2 tablespoons superfine sugar
2 tablespoons rice vinegar
2 tablespoons finely grated gingerroot
2 tablespoons finely grated garlic
2 dried chiles, minced

Mix together all the ingredients for the sauce in a nonreactive shallow dish. Place the chicken in the sauce, turn to coat all over, cover, and let marinate in the refrigerator for up to 1 hour.

Add the oil to a skillet over medium heat. Once the oil is hot, add the chicken, and fry on each side for 4 minutes, or until cooked through, then add all the marinade and bubble up until it is sticky and reduced. Serve, or divide into 4 portions, wrap, and freeze separately. Use 1 portion for a bento box.

Makes 4 bento box portions
776 kcal in total
194 kcal per serving

Chicken teriyaki

The beans and vegetables in this bento box add bulk without heavy carbs or fats.

CHICKEN TERIYAKI

→ See left

EDAMAME RICE

2¾ cups hot, cooked Japanese white rice (see page 20)
½ cup shelled edamame beans

Mix the rice with the edamame. Serve, or divide into 4 portions, wrap, and freeze separately. Use 1 portion for a bento box.

Makes 4 bento box portions
904 kcal in total
226 kcal per serving

GREEN BEANS AND ALMOND BUTTER

I like to use almond butter to bring out the flavor of the beans.

4 teaspoons almond butter
large pinch of superfine sugar
1 teaspoon miso paste
salt
5½ ounces green beans, trimmed

Mix the almond butter in a bowl with the sugar, miso, and salt to taste.

Bring a pan of water to a boil and add salt. Drop in the beans and cook for 3 minutes, until soft.

Drain the beans, toss them in the

bowl with the almond mixture, and mix well.

Serve, or divide into 4 portions, wrap, and freeze separately. Use 1 portion for a bento box.

Makes 4 bento box portions
152 kcal in total
38 kcal per serving

CREAMY PUMPKIN

A healthy but beautifully rich-tasting dish. Filling and great for you.

1 small pumpkin or acorn squash
2 teaspoons sake
2 teaspoons superfine sugar
2 teaspoons mirin
2 teaspoons soy sauce

Remove all the seeds from the pumpkin and cut the flesh into 1¼-inch pieces.

Put it in a pan with 1¾ cups of water and the remaining ingredients, making sure the pumpkin skin is touching the bottom of the pan. Cover the pan and bring to a boil over high heat. Reduce the heat and simmer for 15 minutes.

Remove the lid and cook over medium heat until all the water has evaporated. Serve, or divide into 4 portions, wrap, and freeze separately. Use 1 portion for a bento box.

Makes 4 bento box portions
148 kcal in total
37 kcal per serving

キレイなお弁当

NO. 4
Low-fat protein punch

High in protein, this bento box will fill you up all day.

BROILED SALMON

→ See page 77, Use ½ quantity Broiled Salmon (60g). Use one-half the quantity of salmon you would serve for a Japanese breakfast as a bento box portion.

Makes 1 bento box portion
123 kcal per serving

JAPANESE OMELET WITH CHIVES

→ See page 77. Make the omelet with a generous handful of minced chives. Use 1 serving as a bento box portion.

Makes 1 bento box portion
86 kcal per serving

OIL-FREE MUSHROOM SALAD

→ See page 83. Use 1 serving as a bento box portion.

Makes 1 bento box portion
7.5 kcal per serving

POPEYE SPINACH SALAD

→ See page 89; use 1 serving as a bento box portion

Makes 1 bento box portion
92 kcal per serving

BROWN RICE

→ See page 20. Add 1 cup cooked Japanese brown rice to this bento box.

Makes 1 bento box portion
200 kcal per serving

NO. 5
Sweet chili shrimp

Create a lunch time treat with more exotic ingredients to wake up your taste buds.

SWEET CHILI SHRIMP

Guaranteed to tick all your taste cravings.

10 ounces raw shrimp, deveined

For the marinade
1 teaspoon salt
4 teaspoons sake
4 teaspoons cornstarch
1½ teaspoons sesame oil

For the rest
4 tablespoons tomato ketchup
4 teaspoons miso paste
4 teaspoons superfine sugar
2 teaspoons finely grated gingerroot
2 teaspoons finely grated garlic
2 teaspoons cooking oil
1¼ cups minced scallion
1 teaspoon tobanjan (chili bean sauce, optional)

Place the shrimp in a bowl with all the ingredients for the marinade and mix well.

Mix the tomato ketchup, miso, sugar, ginger, and garlic in another small bowl with scant ½ cup of water.

Add the oil to a skillet over medium heat. Add the scallion and stir well until you can smell it. Add the shrimp and cook, turning, until they are all nice and pink.

Add the ketchup mixture and cook for 3 minutes. Add the tobanjan (if using) and serve. Or divide into 4 portions, wrap, and freeze separately (do *not* refreeze shrimp that were previously frozen). Use 1 portion for a bento box.

Makes 4 bento box portions
632 kcal in total
158 kcal per serving

BROWN RICE

→ See page 20. Add 1 cup cooked Japanese brown rice to this bento box.

Makes 1 bento box portion
191 kcal per serving

ASPARAGUS WITH MUSHROOMS AND SESAME OIL

A really light side dish. The sesame oil gives it an unusual depth.

3 pound asparagus spears
salt
4 teaspoons sesame oil
½ cup mushrooms, finely sliced

Cut the asparagus into ¾-inch pieces. Cook in boiling salted water for 3 minutes. Drain.

Add the sesame oil to a skillet over medium heat. Add the asparagus and mushrooms and stir for 3 minutes, or until the mushrooms are soft. Serve, or divide into 4 portions, wrap, and freeze separately.

Makes 4 bento box portions
224 kcal in total
56 kcal per serving

JAPANESE OMELET WITH EDAMAME OR GREEN PEA

→ See page 77. Make the omelet with 2¼ ounces edamame beans, or peas. Use 1 serving as a bento box portion.

Makes 1 bento box portion
95 kcal per serving

NO. 6
Spicy chicken-and-egg

A great bento for days when you want a treat.

SPICY CHICKEN

If you like heat, this does the trick.

2 tablespoons English mustard
2 teaspoons whole grain mustard
2 teaspoons white wine vinegar
2 teaspoons all-purpose flour
4 teaspoons paprika
4 skinless chicken thighs
(3 ounces each)
salt and freshly ground black pepper
2 teaspoons cooking oil

Mix the 2 mustards, vinegar, flour, and paprika in a bowl. Stab the chicken with a fork all over and season. Paint the mustard sauce over the chicken, cover, and marinate for 30 minutes.

Put a skillet over low heat with the oil. Add the chicken, cover, and cook for 10 minutes, turning once. Serve, or divide into 4 portions, wrap, and freeze separately.

Makes 4 bento box portions
652 kcal in total
163 kcal per serving

BOILED ASPARAGUS

¾ pound trimmed asparagus spears
salt

Cook the asparagus in boiling salted water for 3 minutes, then drain. Serve, or divide into 4 portions, wrap, and freeze separately.

Makes 4 bento box portions
72 kcal in total
18 kcal per serving

BALSAMIC PICKLED EGG

These pickled eggs are simple to make and are a great protein snack.

4 eggs
4 tablespoons balsamic vinegar
4 teaspoons soy sauce
2 teaspoons mirin
2½ tablespoons superfine sugar

Boil the eggs for 7 to 8 minutes. The yolk should remain moist. Peel.

Mix the balsamic, soy, mirin, and sugar in a pan. Heat gently, stirring, until the sugar dissolves.

Put the eggs in a sterilized jar and pour over the hot vinegar. Seal, let cool, then refrigerate for 2 days, turning twice a day, before serving.

Makes 4 bento box portions
492 kcal in total
123 kcal per serving

BROWN RICE

→ See page 20. Add 1 cup cooked Japanese brown rice to this bento box.

Makes 1 bento box portion
200 kcal per serving

キレイなお弁当

NO. 7
Inside-out rolls

A soothing combination of calming green goodies and nurturing fish and egg.

SUSHI (FROZEN SUSHI)

→ Take the sushi rolls from your freezer in the morning, pack them in your bento box, and they will be perfectly defrosted by lunchtime.

JAPANESE OMELET, BEAN, AND CRAB INSIDE-OUT ROLL

→ To make the inside-out rolls, refer to the step-by-step guide (see page 36). Fill with:

¾ ounce Japanese omelet (see page 77)
2 teaspoons Green Beans and Almond Butter (see page 103)
2 crab sticks

Makes 1 roll (6 pieces)
382 kcal

OIL-FREE EDAMAME

→ See page 85; add ½ portion to this bento box.

Makes 1 bento box portion
100 kcal per serving

NO. 8
Salad day

The perfect salad combo bento box for when you want fresh, fresh, fresh! This does what it says on the can and satisfies when you really need to fill up. You can cook the noodles the night before, then add the salad ingredients in the morning. (Or even defrost frozen noodles, see page 87.)

FILL-YOU-UP SOBA NOODLE SALAD

→ See page 87; use 1 serving as a bento box portion

Makes 1 bento box portion
501 kcal per serving

NO. 9
Omega-3 and wasabi veg

A lean and healthy bento, bursting with vitality-boosting ingredients.

SMOKED MACKEREL

2 ounces smoked mackerel, flaked or left whole

130 kcal per serving

JAPANESE OMELET WITH EDAMAME OR GREEN PEA

→ See page 77. Make the omelet with 2¼ ounces of edamame beans, or peas. Use 1 serving as a bento box portion.

Makes 1 bento box portion
95 kcal per serving

MIXED VEGETABLES WITH WASABI DRESSING

8 okra pods
20 green beans, halved
1½ ounces carrot, cut into thin sticks
1 tablespoon Wasabi Dressing (see page 100)

Boil the okra pods, green beans, and carrot for 2 minutes, then drain and mix with the Wasabi Dressing. Serve, or divide into 4 portions, wrap, and freeze separately.

Makes 4 bento box portions
80 kcal in total
20 kcal per serving

WHITE RICE

Add 1 cup cooked Japanese white rice (see page 20) to this bento box.

Makes 1 bento box portion
214 kcal per serving

NO. 10
Inside-out rolls with protein boost

A selection of classic Japanese goodies, to make you the envy of your work colleagues.

SMOKED SALMON AND CUCUMBER INSIDE-OUT ROLL

→ To make the inside-out rolls, refer to the step-by-step guide (see page 36). Fill with:

For the covering
3–4 smoked salmon slices
6 very fine slices of unwaxed lemon

For the filling
2 thin cucumber sticks

Makes 1 roll (6 pieces)
353 kcal

JAPANESE OMELET

→ See page 77. Use 1 serving as a bento box portion.

Makes 1 bento box portion
86 kcal per serving

OIL-FREE EDAMAME

→ See page 85; add ¼ portion to this bento box.

Makes 1 bento box portion
50 kcal per serving

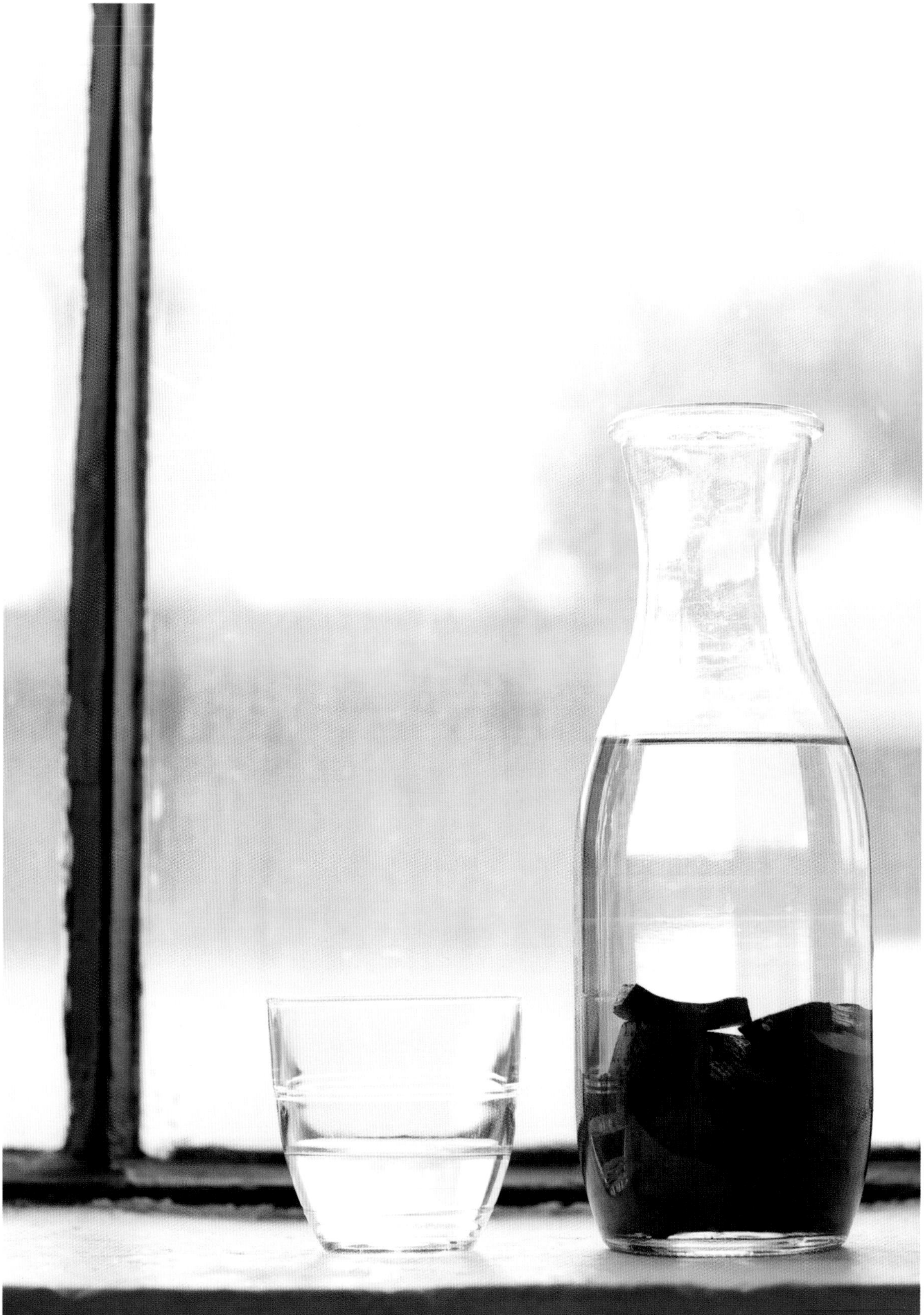

Sushi to impress

Chess sushi
Spring garden
Soba sushi
Treasure in a box
Maki in Spain
Octopus "tacos"

KAISENDON
Seafood special
Tuna medley
Omega-3 bomb
Salmon lover

ELEGANT, STUNNING SPREADS

*These dishes are for special people and magical nights.
Unlike the other recipes in Sushi Slim, you may have to
visit a Japanese store for some of the ingredients.*

Visually stunning and inviting, these sushi spreads are an explosion of color and texture combined with seductive flavors. As you will see in the coming pages, the recipes in this chapter truly pack a huge visual punch, and are perfect for serving at more formal occasions, or when you want to make a big impact. The beautiful sushi tableaux create a party atmosphere. Once made, you can lay them out at the last moment, then you won't have to spend any time in the kitchen away from your guests.

These recipes are not part of the weekly Sushi Slim plan; they are special occasion meals, so I have not included a calorie count. (Though they're healthy and not fattening.) After all, we have to relax every now and then ...

Take this idea as a template and let your imagination run wild. You can make your chess board as big as you want, and you can make it with nigiri and gunkan as well as with hosomaki rolls, but it looks best when you use just one type of sushi.

The finest ingredients set the mood for a special evening or celebration. This sushi gets its name from the flower-style shapes it creates. As always, all the fish needs to be sushi-grade. We eat this in springtime, to celebrate the season.

A rice-free roll stuffed instead with buckwheat noodles. Unusual, filling, and tasty.

CHESS SUSHI
Pictured left

Four types:
cucumber
avocado and chili
salmon
tuna

To make the hosomaki rolls, refer to the step-by-step guide (see page 31), using the fillings on pages 32–35.

Serve with soy sauce, pickled ginger, and wasabi paste.

Makes as much as you want

SPRING GARDEN
Pictured on page 114

For the yellowtail "flower"
3½ ounces skinned yellowtail fillet
1 shiso leaf, or arugula leaf

For the salmon "flower"
3½ ounces skinned salmon fillet
1 king scallop
1 shiso leaf, or arugula leaf

For the scallop "flower"
2 king scallops
1 tablespoon salmon roe

Cut the yellowtail and salmon into very fine slices on the diagonal, against the grain. Slice the king scallops for the scallop "flower" 5 times horizontally. Cut the scallop for the salmon "flower" into strips.

Put a shiso leaf on 2 of 3 plates. Arrange the yellowtail and salmon slices on the plates into flower shapes, treating each slice as a petal, wrapping them around each other. Fill the salmon "flower" with scallop strips.

Arrange the scallop slices on the third plate as the petals of a flower, placing the salmon roe in the middle.

Serve with soy sauce, pickled ginger, and wasabi paste.

Each "flower" serves 1

SOBA SUSHI
Pictured on page 115

1¼ ounces soba noodles (cooked weight)
3 tablespoons Tempura Sauce (see page 40)
½ sheet of nori seaweed (halved horizontally)

Bring 3½ quarts of water to a boil and cook the soba noodles for 15 minutes (or according to the package directions). Drain, then rinse the noodles under cold water. Drain really well once more.

Dress the noodles with the Tempura Sauce, tossing them to coat.

To make the hosomaki rolls, refer to the step-by-step guide (see page 31). Line the noodles up along 1 long side of the nori, straightening them out as far as possible. Cut the roll evenly into 6 pieces, wiping the knife blade between cuts.

Serve with soy sauce, pickled ginger, and wasabi paste.

Makes 6 pieces

Show your artistic flair with these little Japanese-style wraps.

The addition of air-dried ham to these rolls, using it in place of nori seaweed, gives an unexpected and toothsome twist.

These are little mouthfuls of spiciness.

TREASURE IN A BOX

Pictured left

For the egg crepe
2 eggs, beaten
½ teaspoon superfine sugar
pinch of salt
¼ teaspoon flavorless oil

For the filling
¼ ounce skinless salmon fillet
3 or 4 green beans, trimmed
¼ cucumber, seeded
¼ avocado, peeled and pitted
2 tablespoons chopped bamboo shoot, boiled if fresh
2 or 3 shiitake mushrooms, trimmed
½ cup prepared and seasoned sushi rice (see page 20)

To finish
4 cooked shrimp (see page 40), halved lengthwise
8 x 2½-inch lengths of chive

Mix together the eggs, sugar, and salt, and heat the oil in a 12-inch skillet. Add the egg batter and swirl the pan to coat the bottom. When it has set, flip the crepe and cook the other side for 30 seconds. Remove from the pan.

For the filling, cut everything except the rice into ¼-inch cubes. Mix them evenly through the rice.

Cut the crepe into 4 quarter circles. Place one-quarter of the rice mixture in the center of each piece of crepe. Wrap as you would a present, to enclose the filling in a neat box.

Arrange on a platter, adding 2 shrimp halves and 2 chive lengths to each.

Makes 4 pieces

MAKI IN SPAIN

Pictured on page 118

¾ ounce sliced Serrano ham
2 avocado slices
2–3 shiso leaves, or arugula leaves
5 chives
¾ cup prepared and seasoned sushi rice (see page 20)

To make the rolls, refer to the step-by-step guide for hosomaki (see page 31), using ham in place of nori seaweed, and the avocado, shiso, and chives as the filling.

Makes 6 pieces

OCTOPUS "TACOS"

Pictured on page 119

2 tablespoons all-purpose flour
1 tablespoon chili powder, ideally Japanese chili powder
½ tablespoon sea salt
1½ ounces octopus, cut into ⅝-inch chunks
sunflower oil, to deep-fry
4 lettuce leaves
wafer-thin cucumber slices and shredded scallion, to serve

Mix the flour, chili powder, and salt in a shallow dish. Add the octopus chunks and toss to coat well. Cover and set aside for 30 minutes, for the flavors to get to know each other.

Heat the sunflower oil in a deep, heavy pan until it reaches 350°F on an oil thermometer.

Fry the pieces of octopus, being careful not to crowd the pan, for 3 to 4 minutes, turning once, until nicely golden brown. Remove with a slotted spoon and drain briefly on paper towels, to remove excess oil.

Lay the lettuce leaves on a platter and scatter a few slices of cucumber into each. Divide the octopus between the lettuce cups, and sprinkle each with scallion. Serve immediately.

Makes 4 tacos

KAISENDON

Dishes of sashimi laid over seasoned sushi rice, this is opulent special occasion food, and worth a trip to a Japanese store. As ever, all the fish needs to be sushi-grade.

A stunning, simple yet extravagant dish to share with friends. See page 24 for how to cut fish for sashimi.

One for the connoisseur, this contrasts slices of tuna from different parts of the fish, each prized for its unique qualities.

SEAFOOD SPECIAL
Pictured left, below

1½ cups just-prepared seasoned sushi rice (see page 20)
2 cooked shrimp (see page 40)
4 sashimi slices sea bream
4 sashimi slices tuna
4 sashimi slices salmon
4 sashimi slices yellowtail
4 sashimi slices surf clam
1 shiso leaf, or arugula leaf

Spoon the rice into an attractive bowl. It should still have a breath of warmth to it.

Lay on the shrimp and the fish, grouping the same type together and arranging them in a circular pattern on the rice. Add the shiso leaf.

Serve with soy sauce, pickled ginger, and wasabi paste. Sake makes an excellent accompanying drink.

Serves 1 generously

TUNA MEDLEY
Pictured left, above

1½ cups just-prepared seasoned sushi rice (see page 20)
6 sashimi slices tuna loin (maguro)
4 sashimi slices medium-fatty tuna (chutoro)
3 sashimi slices fatty tuna (otoro)
2 shiso leaves, or arugula leaves

Spoon the rice into an attractive bowl. It should still have a breath of warmth to it.

Lay on the slices of tuna, keeping the same type together and arranging them in lines. Add the shiso leaves, using them to separate each type of tuna.

Serve with soy sauce, pickled ginger, and wasabi paste. Eat it with sake or shochu.

Serves 1 generously

An impressive way to prepare and present home-marinated fish at the table.

Salmon tends to be everyone's favorite sushi and sashimi fish, so this is a good choice to serve to sushi novices.

OMEGA-3 BOMB
Pictured right, below

1½ cups just-prepared seasoned sushi rice (see page 20)
2 fillets Marinated Mackerel
(see page 59)
1 shiso leaf, or arugula leaf
4 small slices surf clam (optional)

Spoon the rice into an attractive bowl. It should still have a breath of warmth to it.

Cut the mackerel into neat slices and lay it over the rice, retaining the shape of the fillets as far as possible. Arrange the shiso leaf and surf clam (if using) together, over the fish.

Serve with soy sauce, pickled ginger, and wasabi paste. Sake makes an excellent accompanying drink.

Serves 1 generously

SALMON LOVER
Pictured right, above

1½ cups just-prepared seasoned sushi rice (see page 20)
12 sashimi slices salmon
1 king scallop
1 tablespoon salmon roe

Spoon the rice into an attractive bowl. It should still have a breath of warmth to it.

Lay the salmon over the rice in a circular pattern. Slice the scallop horizontally 5 times, and arrange the slices in the center of the bowl. Top with the salmon roe.

Serve with soy sauce, pickled ginger, and wasabi paste. Eat it with sake or shochu.

Serves 1 generously

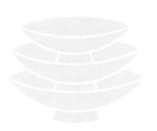

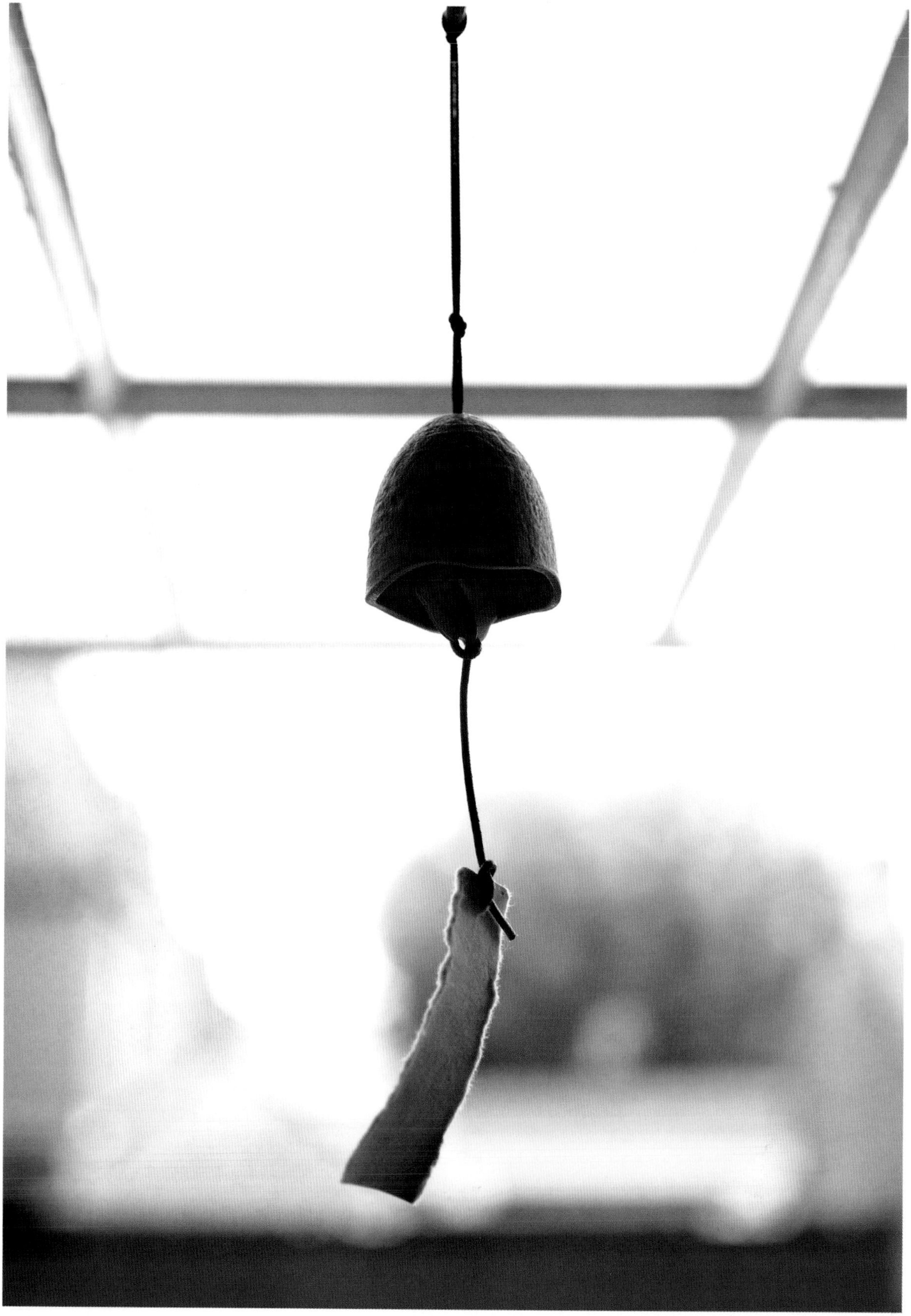

Index

I would like to thank Diana, Anne, and Helen for giving me a chance to publish this book. Without them, Sushi Slim would not exist.

To Lucy for her patience and great support. To Lisa for the gorgeous pictures that brought my recipes to life. To Risa for her design and suggestions. To Miki Symons, for her painstaking counting of every calorie in this book!

To Emma for lending me the amazing experience she has collected in her career, and for being there for me for all these years.

To Andrea, Haru, Mai, and all Suzu's members for their presence and support.

To my parents Mamoru and Motoko, and my children Eleanor, Leon, Suzu, and Verity, for inspiring me and bringing happiness into my life.

And finally, to Simon Matthews, for supporting me all this time and helping me to get this far.

Editorial Director Anne Furniss
Creative Director Helen Lewis
Project Editor Lucy Bannell
Art Direction and Design Mentsen
Photography Lisa Linder
Editorial Consultant Emma Bannister
Dietitian Miki Symons
Food Styling Aya Nishimura
Production Leonie Kellman, Vincent Smith

First published in 2013 by
Quadrille Publishing Ltd
www.quadrille.co.uk

Text © 2013 by Makiko Sano
Photography © 2013 by Lisa Linder
Design & layout © 2013 by Quadrille
Publishing Ltd

Published by The Countryman Press,
P.O. Box 748, Woodstock, VT 05091

Distributed by W. W. Norton & Company, Inc.,
500 Fifth Avenue, New York, NY 10110

Printed in China

10 9 8 7 6 5 4 3 2 1

Printed in China.